The Beatitudes from the Back Side

J. ELLSWORTH KALAS

Abingdon Press
NASHVILLE

THE BEATITUDES FROM THE BACK SIDE

Copyright © 2008 by Abingdon Press

This book is printed on acid-free paper.

Library of Congress Cataloging-in-Publication Data

Kalas, J. Ellsworth, 1923-
   The beatitudes from the back side / J. Ellsworth Kalas.
      p. cm.
   Includes bibliographical references.
   ISBN 978-0-687-65084-2 (binding: adhesive, perfect : alk. paper)
   1. Beatitudes. I. Title.

BT382.K35 2008
241.5'3—dc22

2007040267

08 09 10 11 12 13 14 15 16 17—10 9 8 7 6 5 4 3 2 1

MANUFACTURED IN THE UNITED STATES OF AMERICA

To Stephen Ellsworth Clines
May you always know how much God loves you

CONTENTS

CHAPTER 1

A Declaration of Dependence

Some years ago, during a church conference in California, the Reverend Faith Conklin approached me in a bookstore to thank me for the books I have written. She then went on to suggest a book she hoped I would write someday. I was grateful for both words. Authors don't have that many opportunities to talk with the persons who have read their books, so a word of thanks is always welcome. But so, too, is an idea for another book because often readers know better than authors what people are interested in reading.

"I wish you'd do another book with your 'Back Side' approach," she said. "The Beatitudes from the Back Side." I agreed readily that it was a good idea, but I explained that it was also a very difficult one.

It's not only that the Beatitudes—a series of blessings spoken by Jesus—are a challenging subject; the point is that they're *already* "from the back side." If we approach the Beatitudes just the way they appear in the Sermon on the Mount (see Matthew 5:3-12; Luke 6:20-23), we discover within the first sentence that we are looking at things in a manner utterly at odds with our usual outlook on life. From where we generally live out our lives, the Beatitudes seem so contrary as to be coming from "the back side."

And all the more so because of their key word, *blessed.* This is a very upbeat word. The synonyms for the particular Greek word that is used in the New Testament include "supremely blest," "fortunate," "happy." In the late William Barclay's translation of the New Testament, that fascinating British scholar began each sentence, not with "blessed," but with "O the bliss!"

Ironically, therefore, the Beatitudes are introduced to us with the kind of language we love in the Western world. Anything that has to do with happiness is the stuff on which advertisers and sales executives build their careers. And of course in America we see such a life as our divine right so that we've written it into our Declaration of Independence: We believe that humans "are endowed, by their Creator, with certain unalienable Rights, that among these are Life, Liberty, and the pursuit of Happiness." We think we not only have a right to happiness, we even have a right to pursue it.

But when we start examining the Beatitudes we realize that in Jesus' view happiness is not something we get by pursuing it; indeed, almost the contrary. We're told that we will be happy—or blessed, if you prefer—in what appears to be the near antithesis of happiness. If we choose to live by the Beatitudes, we make a declaration of dependence. We put ourselves in bondage to such things as poverty of spirit, purity of heart, and a readiness for persecution. This isn't the sort of product they advertise on prime-time television; indeed, I'm not sure that it appears overly often in our prime-time worship services. That is because this is not a spiritual quick fix. It doesn't come in a five-easy-lessons capsule. Instead, it is largely contrary to the way we live and to the way we think.

Before we go any further, however, let me say that over the past twenty centuries a very great many people have found in these Beatitudes a depth of peace and joy beyond anything our common culture promotes and seeks. But it isn't easy, and it isn't obvious. And although I intend to do my best with this book, I'm not sure you'll buy into the Beatitudes after you've finished your reading. I say this because even as the author, I struggle to live up to what in my heart I know is true.

I suppose that this is partly because I'm looking for logic in the Beatitudes—that is, logic as I define it. Something in me wants to know why the poor in spirit are blessed, and why or how the meek will inherit the earth. And can you really guarantee that the merciful will receive mercy? I think I've seen some merciful people who, it seems, were exploited because they were so merciful.

The Beatitudes form the introduction to what is no doubt the best-known sermon ever preached. We call it the Sermon on the Mount, and of course it was preached by Jesus. We'll talk more about that later. Just now I want to confess my fascination with the way this sermon begins, because if we have read the New Testament just a bit, the Beatitudes catch us off guard. The Gospel of Matthew tells us that when Jesus began his ministry, he said (in the same style as John the Baptist), "Repent, for the kingdom of heaven has come near" (Matthew 4:17). *Repent* is not a happy-sounding word. There's a condemnatory quality to it, as if the judge were saying "guilty" before you've even presented your case.

The Beatitudes, by contrast, begin in a wonderfully positive way. Listen to these opening words from the Sermon on the Mount: "Jesus saw the crowds and went up a hill, where he sat down. His disciples gathered around him, and he began to teach them: '*Happy* are those who . . .' " (Matthew 5:1-3 GNT, emphasis added). That's how Jesus began. Not "Repent," not "Be sorry," not even "Do" or "Be," but "*Happy*." At first hearing, you might think Jesus was changing his approach from the earlier preaching, as if he were trying to be more audience-friendly. But by the end of each sentence you realize that our Lord's message is basically as unsettling as ever—and as contrary to much of our usual thinking. He does want us to know, however, that the way he invites us to join him is ultimately and dramatically a blessed and happy one. He does not pretend that it is easy, but it *is* blessed.

I suspect that most of us need to work on a better definition of *happiness*. The word has its problems, of course. *Happy* is built on the root word *hap*, which means "chance"—as when we say *happen* or *happenstance*. This would make it seem as if happiness were a gamble, and perhaps with bad odds at that. But the Beatitudes are in no way chancy; there is no sense of uncertainty in them. Jesus said, "Happy are . . ." and he added no qualifying phrase such as "in many instances," "given the right circumstances," or "in certain age or economic groups."

Around the middle of the twentieth century, Henry C. Link, at the time probably America's best-known psychologist, came back to the Christian faith. In his book *The Return to Religion*, he took issue with those who measured the abundant life in terms of dollars and the things money can buy. He called such thinking "the most disastrous and destroying ideal which could possibly be offered"; his long years of experience with well-to-do clients were evidence of that. The abundant life, Dr. Link said, "can only be defined in terms of habits, that is, character."[1]

That fits perfectly with the mood of the Beatitudes. These rules of life have nothing to do with have and have-not, or with any circumstances of life, but with character—or perhaps to put it another way, with our very structures of living.

William Barclay, the British Bible scholar to whom I referred earlier, is helpful at this point. He tells us that the word in our Greek New Testament that is translated as "blessed" or "happy" is the word the Greeks used to describe the island of Cyprus. They call it *he makaria*—that is, "the Happy Isle." They felt that Cyprus was so beautiful and so rich in resources, and so fertile, that a person would never need to go beyond its coastline to find everything he or she needed for perfect happiness. Professor Barclay then went on to say, "*Makarios* then describes that joy which has its secret within itself, that joy which is serene and untouchable, and self-contained . . . completely independent of all the chances and changes of life."[2]

So when we say that the **Beatitudes** describe the **happy life**, we are speaking of a very special kind of happiness. It has little or nothing to do with chance or circumstances, and it doesn't depend on health or wealth or even achievements. It is (as the Greeks perceived the island of Cyprus) *complete within itself.* One doesn't need to go beyond its borders to fulfill the quest.

Thus, the happiness of which I speak—contrary to its root word—doesn't depend on *happenings.* It is not a gamble. The person at the racetrack calculates his odds on matters such as the condition of the track, the skill of the jockey, and the mood of the horse on that particular day. The financial consultant calculates the volatility of the market. The farmer has to be concerned not only with the weather but, at season's end, with the price in the marketplace. But there are no odds to be reckoned with in the Beatitudes. They offer a happiness that has no *hap.*

Our Lord demonstrated this quality of happiness during his earthly ministry. On the night of his betrayal—perhaps within the hour itself—Jesus told his disciples that the time had come "when you will be scattered, each one to his home, and you will leave me alone. Yet I am not alone. . . . In the world you face persecution. But take courage; I have conquered the world!" (John 16:32-33). It hardly looked that way. The world, in the form of Roman soldiers accompanied by one of Jesus' former disciples, came to Jesus' garden of prayer, hustled him through mock trials and sundry abuse, and in little more than a dozen hours had him at the place of crucifixion. But he had conquered, no doubt about it. The people who are best remembered from the first century A.D. are those persons who are remembered either for allying with Jesus or for opposing him. He is the polestar around whom the rest of the world has since then found its significance. No wonder, then, that the supposed dying words of the Roman emperor Julian the Apostate— "You have won, Galilean"—have become a symbol of the continuing conquering power of Christ.

But I think I would not find so much strength and consolation in the example of our Lord if I had not seen the same qualities in the lives of everyday persons I have known. Otherwise I might say that the living-out of the Beatitudes is possible only for the divine, when in fact Jesus has given his followers and potential followers the promise that this is the kind of life he offers to all who will follow him, including you and me. "I have conquered the world." No need, then, to be afraid.

Most of us have known someone whose happiness had nothing to do with chance, with *hap*. I've been thinking this week of a farm woman from my first congregation, Tillie Roth. Tillie had never married; I think she was in her mid-fifties, but since I was barely thirty at the time I was not too adept at judging ages of those half a generation or more beyond me. Tillie was always a delight. Greeting her before or after a worship service or some other church event was an unfailing reason for laughter. It wasn't that she had some store of jokes; it was simply that she exuded goodwill; I always began smiling involuntarily when I saw her approaching.

Then, quite without warning, she was diagnosed with cancer. The malignancy took over her body with breakneck speed. She would apologize as soon as I visited her because there was an odor of decay in her room, but once that formality was out of the way she was the same fun Tillie I had always known. She was going down, but she was far from out. She would not, as Dylan Thomas phrased it, "go gentle" into the night, but neither would she rage against it.

Instead, she mocked it. It was not that she issued any grand statements; it was simply very clear that death had no dominion over her. Since her happiness didn't come from or depend upon chance or circumstances, it remained undiminished. Indeed, if anything, her happiness seemed at times to gain strength even as her body decayed, as if her happiness fed on the stuff that sought to destroy her.

Since then I've known more than one Tillie Roth, people who continued to be owned by blessedness even as they were in the territory of presumed disaster. At another level, I've been impressed by those who aren't undone by what so many consider the tedium of life; they find gladness and laughter in life's ordinariness. So many in our culture pursue diversion and distraction as if life itself were something to be hurried through in a preoccupied state. They don't so much live their days as avoid them. By contrast, the people of faith of whom I am speaking have a remarkable grasp on life. C. S. Lewis said that his mother "had the talent for happiness in a high degree—went straight for it as the experienced travelers go for the best seat in a train."[3] Or as William Barclay put it, the Beatitudes are not "nebulous prophecies of some future bliss; they are congratulations on what is."[4]

I like that! Congratulations on what *is*. I believe in heaven, but just now I'm living on this planet, and by God's grace I don't want to wish this life away or to get through it as quickly as possible. And for sure, I don't want simply to endure it or to seek to prolong it only because I fear what may follow it. The Beatitudes are for living this life now, in the midst of the *is*. And the Beatitudes have been given to us for life on this earth. They may indeed strike us as impractical, but perhaps that's because our definition of *practical* or *realistic* is so one-dimensional. A way of life that works only at the most superficial levels isn't worthy of eternal creatures—and never forget that you and I are eternal creatures. Nor can we be satisfied with a philosophy of life that bends or breaks when tested. And especially, we shouldn't be content with a life or a presumed faith that simply endures this life. I surely wouldn't trust eternity to a God who gave us a life on this planet that was only to be endured and survived!

So we look for a life—and a Lord of life—that takes life captive, whatever and however it is. A life that, by God's grace, is *blessed. Happy. Not held by chance.*

But we need to know from the beginning of our study that many of our old definitions will suffer demolition as we explore this beatific life. Did you expect that word, *beatific?* You should have, of course, since it is a first cousin of *Beatitude.* But do you remember its definition? "Beatitude: bestowing bliss, blessings, happiness, or the like."[5] That's what the Beatitudes offer: a beatific life.

But here's the back side. This happiness is not by way of any Declaration of Independence, admirable as that document is. Rather, this happiness comes by our personal declaration of *dependence.* It is the magnificent trust in God that the medieval nun Julian of Norwich expressed when she declared that "all shall be well, and all shall be well, and all manner of thing shall be well."

But contrary to what you might think, there's nothing easy or soft about this kind of dependence. Rather, it is an attitude that demands a huge store of courage. It's the kind of dependence the trapeze artist displays when he or she lets go of the bar and with no safety net awaiting, flies off into space, trusting.

So, welcome to the Beatitudes. And may you be eternally happy, beginning now. 11|08

CHAPTER *2*

The Place, the People, and the Preacher

When you read Matthew, Mark, Luke, and John, the four little books that tell us almost everything we know about the most enchanting person who ever walked on our planet, you realize that you're reading not an organized textbook but the report of people who were fascinated by what they had seen and heard. A man named Jesus of Nazareth, who had been a village carpenter until he was thirty years old, had become a wandering teacher. He spent the better part of three years in a land about the size of the state of New Jersey, only rarely going beyond its borders. Most of the time the people who made up his audience were "the people of the land," the common folk who spent their lives simply working to keep alive. Occasionally a rich person came to him, and once a devout scholar named Nicodemus, but generally those other than the common folk were the infamous—despised tax collectors, public sinners, the ailing, and the oppressed. The small group who eventually affiliated themselves with him for concentrated study were mostly small-business people—what today we would call owners of mom-and-pop stores, except that in their case they were fishermen or tax collectors or without specific identification.

9

Jesus was known popularly as both a miracle worker and a teacher. If I know human nature, I suspect that those who were drawn to him came first because of the miracles—especially the healings, and the deliverance of those who were so beleaguered that people said they had demons—and that the best of those who came then stayed in order to hear him teach and preach. I venture they reasoned that if a person could do the things Jesus did, he must possess some gift or power or purity that made him closer to God than anyone they had ever seen, so they wanted to know his secrets, as outlined in his teachings.

But for us, his followers and students some twenty centuries later, I've used the wrong word when I refer to an "outline" of his teachings. As I said at the outset of this chapter, what we know about Jesus hasn't come to us by way of an organized textbook; rather, we have these almost casual but wonderfully exciting reports from eyewitnesses or from persons to whom the eyewitnesses gave their information. In most cases, therefore, Jesus' story comes to us as a mixture of events and lessons. Sometimes the lessons stand alone, but sometimes they emerge from the events themselves. But in almost no case is a lesson structured the way we expect teaching to be.

Several times in the Gospel of Matthew, however, a number of related lessons are brought together in one place. The most notable of these is what generations have called the Sermon on the Mount (see Matthew 5:1–7:29). The Beatitudes—the series of quite enigmatic descriptions of the happy life—form an introduction to this sermon.

We call it, as I've just said, a *sermon*. I dare say it is the most famous discourse ever delivered at any time or any place. I say this as one who admires the art of public address. As such I revel in the achievements of Disraeli, Gladstone, and Winston Churchill, and hundreds of lesser-known figures whose speeches and sermons have stirred people over the centuries of human history. I think especially of particular speeches for particular occasions—like Lincoln's Gettysburg Address, or President Franklin Delano Roosevelt's speech after the bombing of Pearl Harbor. Yet, as great as these addresses were, they can't fairly be compared in their influence on the human race with the speech that we call the Sermon on the Mount.

And ponder this. So many of the great orations that have played a part in the shaping of history were energized by the occasion for which or within which they were given. The power of a State of the Union address or of Winston Churchill's classic wartime speeches came in some measure from the occasions on which they were delivered. The Sermon on the Mount, on the other hand, had no such external factor to give it significance. It must have been an altogether ordinary day in Palestine, without fanfare or gravitas. The audience (which we will discuss shortly) brought no distinction to the occasion. The occasion added nothing to the speech; instead, the speech made the occasion. Some ordinary people came on an ordinary day to a place of no previous significance, and for the centuries that have followed, the audience and the setting (even though we cannot fully identify it) are part of history. The message and the messenger made it so. I suspect no one can estimate faithfully the number of languages into which the Sermon on the Mount has been translated, or the books that have analyzed, praised, or contended with it—to say nothing of course of the tens of thousands of sermons that are preached from it every year, in essentially every part of the world.

And yet when we read this sermon we discover that it doesn't claim to be a sermon. The Bible says simply that Jesus "began to speak, and taught them, saying . . ." (Matthew 5:2). In other words, this was not so much a sermon or a speech, as a teacher instructing a class. I don't really know why we call these three chapters of Matthew's Gospel a sermon rather than a lesson; perhaps some long-ago preachers decided to lay claim to the title because as preachers they thought that anything so wonderful had to be not simply a lesson, but a sermon.

So where was it delivered? If you travel in the land of Israel today, your tour guide will almost surely include on your itinerary a visit to a beautiful spot that he will identify as the place traditionally considered to be the place where Jesus delivered this sermon. The biblical record doesn't give us any real clue concerning the location. Matthew tells us that Jesus had been going "throughout Galilee, teaching," and that "his fame spread throughout all Syria," and that "great crowds followed him from Galilee, the Decapolis, Jerusalem, Judea, and from beyond the Jordan" (Matthew 4:23-25). Only then does the writer say, "When Jesus saw the crowds, he went up the mountain; and after he sat down, his disciples came to him. Then he began to speak, and taught them, saying"—and the famed sermon begins (Matthew 5:1-2).

So we don't really know where the mountain was. I can promise you that it wasn't a towering promontory, like one would find in the Alps or the Rockies or the Himalayan mountains. Israel's mountains are relatively small—sometimes rough and certainly rocky, but more like what we often describe as foothills. This particular spot no doubt provided a kind of small, natural amphitheater, a place where the speaker was easily visible and where the voice would carry without any amplification other than what the setting itself provided.

Appropriately, it was a *high* place; not so high as to be inaccessible, but high enough that one felt psychologically lifted. Settings influence our experiences, and this setting had a kind of upward pull. But there is something symbolically right about this sermon being associated with a mountain, because its message has such an insistent upward intention. I still sing a favorite prayer-meeting song of my childhood, that began with the affirmation, "I'm pressing on the upward way, / new heights I'm gaining every day," and pleading repeatedly for "higher ground."[1] The setting for the Sermon on the Mount is itself a kind of object lesson for the message given there. It is a "mountain top experience," a lifelong call to go up higher. Perhaps by this time you've been struck by what may or may not be a significant similarity with the Old Testament. Moses received the Ten Commandments on a mountain, Sinai, and now Jesus gives what might be called his keynote address on a mountain. Early biblical scholars, including Augustine, Jerome, Chrysostom, and Chromatius, saw a relationship between the two stories. I especially like these words from Chromatius: "The severity of the law was first given by Moses on the mountain, but the people were forbidden to draw close. Now with Jesus, all are invited to draw near to him to hear of the gift of the gospel."[2]

Jesus' followers over the centuries have seen the Sermon on the Mount as addressed to them, at least in a general way. But who constituted the first audience? Matthew describes the scene this way: "When Jesus saw the crowds, he went up the mountain; and after he sat down, his disciples came to him." And it is after they had come to him that Jesus "began to speak, and taught them" (Matthew 5:1-2). And yet, as the sermon ends, Matthew writes, "Now when Jesus had finished saying these things, the *crowds* were astounded at his teaching, for he taught them as one having authority, and not as their scribes" (Matthew 7:28-29, emphasis added).

So to whom was the Sermon on the Mount originally given, to the disciples or to a great crowd? My own impression, for whatever its worth, is that the disciples were gathered close to our Lord—just as you might expect them to be, not only because the disciples would insist on being close but also because the crowds would make way for Jesus' students—and the crowds stayed close enough to listen in. Obviously they listened closely enough and with enough personal involvement to get the impact of what Jesus had been saying, so that they were astounded by it.

I suspect this is something of a microcosm of what has happened all through the centuries of our Lord's kingdom. A small group—what Jesus might call the leaven, or the mustard seed—is close at hand, not physically but spiritually—while the mass of people listen at more of a distance. Now the hope, of course, is this: that from those listening out in the crowd some will move up into the circle of the disciples. I venture that perhaps among those in the crowd that day were some who later became part of the seventy who were commissioned by our Lord (see Luke 10:1-24); and indeed, that perhaps some in that crowd were among the hundred and twenty who received the Holy Spirit on the Day of Pentecost (see Acts 1–2).

Of this I am very sure: the Sermon delivered so long ago is intended for all who are willing to receive it. Through the grace of God and the faithfulness of the early witnesses, the New Testament has come to our world over these twenty centuries. Millions beyond numbering have heard. Some have chosen to move up closer, into the body of commitment that we call believers, while others have stayed at a somewhat safe distance (though no one is ever really safe from conversion who has heard a word from our Lord); and there is always some movement from the larger number into the smaller one—and also, I regret to say, from the smaller number back into the more casual, uncommitted group. The journey into God's kingdom isn't always the structured, tidy affair we'd like it to be.

As for those who are in the circle of commitment, the disciples: they too (or *we* too, if I may speak for you and me) are at different levels of intimacy with our Lord. Jesus made this abundantly clear when he selected Peter, James, and John to be a kind of inner circle. I think this is also a factor in the memorable instance where Jesus seemed to side with Mary when her sister Martha complained that Mary was leaving her with all the work; Jesus' reply suggests that Mary was right in wanting to go deeper with her faith (see Luke

10:38-42). So in this audience that first heard the Sermon on the Mount, we have a picture of the church in all ages and times. Some are at the far edges of the crowd, and we're not sure that they ever come any closer. Others are so near that we suspect they eventually become part of the closest and most vigorous body of believers. But even within the sacred circle—symbolized in the New Testament by the Twelve—there are still various levels of dedication, perceptiveness, and effectiveness.

And of course that's very much what this study of the Beatitudes is all about. The ultimate goal is not simply to gain a better intellectual grasp of what Jesus meant when he left us with these strange and challenging statements, but to help each of us grow into the fullness of discipleship that our Lord covets for all who claim his name. I suspect that not many of us would declare that we have mastered the life of the Beatitudes. Before we're done, I hope all of us will have made new steps in that direction.

And who was the preacher? That's simple, we answer; and as soon as we answer—at least, as soon as we get past saying simply "Jesus"—we discover that our answer isn't really that simple. When some say "Jesus," they mean God incarnate, as described in the Gospel of John or in Paul's dramatic language in Ephesians, Colossians, and Philippians, for example. Others, however, mean a revered teacher, the ultimate ethicist and the founder of one of the world's great religions.

In the end, you and I must answer that question for ourselves. But for a moment let's consider the feelings of the people who first heard this sermon. I'm quite sure their reactions to Jesus were very far-ranging. Don't be shocked when I say that some probably were bored and left before the sermon was over—especially since many in the crowd were standing, which made exiting easy. Others were impressed, but without much follow-through—much like those persons Jesus described in his parable of the sower as people with whom the seed sprang up quickly, only to die just as quickly. Some said he was a fascinating teacher, and for a while they came to hear him often, and urged others to do so, too. And some said, "Never have I heard anyone speak like this man," and they could not bear to leave him.

Some scholars feel that Matthew 5–7 wasn't really a sermon given on a particular occasion, but rather a collection of Jesus' teachings that the author of this Gospel brought together in organized fashion after our Lord's death. Personally, I'm very content to take Matthew's word for it that there was a day in Jesus' ministry when he spoke his vision of the kingdom as we read it in these chapters. I am also convinced that Jesus spoke most of these teachings, parables, and metaphors on numbers of other occasions— indeed, as we see them scattered in a number of places throughout Luke's Gospel. Any teacher who feels he or she has something worthwhile to say is going to say it more than once. Without a doubt Jesus repeated his basic teachings again and again as he taught in the villages, walked the roads, and stood by the Sea of Galilee.

And now it is ours, to bless and inspire us; and especially, to challenge us. Some of us, as we look at the introduction to this sermon in the Beatitudes, will keep the material at a safe intellectual distance, where we can speculate on its meaning from a philosophical point of view without being compelled to live it out in our daily lives. Others of us will nod our heads in earnest agreement, but this nodding will be the extent of our action.

But some of us, please God, will say, "I believe this is the kind of life to which the Son of God calls his followers. I don't begin to understand everything that is being asked of me, but I intend to obey what I can grasp and to seek to know still more. And I believe that those who follow our Lord with such a heart are the truly blessed, truly *happy* ones." ₁₁/₁₈

CHAPTER *3*

The humble

Poor and Happy

"Blessed are the poor in Spirit, for theirs is the Kingdom of heaven."

Read Matthew 5:3.

*P*oor is a four-letter word. It doesn't have the obscene quality that we usually associate with that "four-letter word" phrase, but neither is it a word we want attached to ourselves or our way of life. Some of us who grew up poor or who have known some period of poverty sometimes romanticize the experience. But I haven't met many who, when fondly recalling those bygone days, decide to give away what they have so they can enjoy such poverty again. Someone has said, "I've been poor and I've been rich, and I can tell you that I'd rather be rich." That's probably the way most of us think, including those whose comparison is only between being poor and not-quite-so-poor.

So when the first Beatitude begins, "How happy are the poor," we may wait for the end of the sentence, but we're already pretty well prejudiced about whatever will follow. Poverty just isn't pretty. We seek to escape it, not to embrace it. It may look lovely on Francis of Assisi, but it isn't the goal we've set for our lives. It's clear that Jesus wasn't playing to the desires of his listeners when he said,

"How happy are the poor in spirit; / theirs is the kingdom of heaven" (Matthew 5:3 JB). Happy because we're *poor*? That just isn't natural. Of course it isn't. If we are to believe that some kind of poverty, whether of spirit, health, friendship, or money, brings happiness, we'll have to see things differently than we do now.

I should interrupt myself for a moment to remind you of a simple word in the title of this chapter. Please note that it isn't "poor *but* happy," as if we can expect to be happy in spite of our circumstances; rather, it's "poor *and* happy," suggesting that the two words belong together and that it isn't incongruous to link them.

Sometimes we teachers and preachers, when looking at New Testament passages, find help by looking into the Greek, the language in which the New Testament was originally written, because sometimes the Greek puts a word in new and different light. Not this time. In fact, the Greek only makes the situation more difficult. Professor William Barclay tells us that the Greek has two words for *poor*. The first describes a person who has to work for his living; he has nothing to spare, but neither is he destitute. This, however, isn't the word that is used in this Beatitude. The second word, *ptochos*, describes absolute and abject poverty. It comes from a root word meaning "to crouch" or "to cower." You get the picture: this word describes a person whose poverty has beaten him or her to his or her knees; that is, someone who has nothing at all. And this is the word that the New Testament uses. Literally, then, the first Beatitude could read, "Happy is the person who is absolutely destitute."

But of course as this Beatitude appears in Matthew's Gospel, it carries a defining phrase. It doesn't praise poverty in general, but a special kind of poverty: "Happy are the poor *in spirit*." At first that may seem to take some sting from the statement. But if you think a moment longer, you realize that the message is now even more unnerving.

Because, you see, in a sense it is poverty of spirit that we want most to escape. One of the reasons, for instance, for escaping economic poverty is because lack of money seems to force subservience and humiliation on us. "If I had a few million," your neighbor says, "I'd tell the whole world where to go." We want to be free of financial poverty so we can escape the poverty of spirit.

You notice, of course, that I am interpreting "spirit" in more than the restricted religious sense. Mind you, the religious element is still a factor; indeed, the determining factor. But as you well know, our culture speaks often of spirit with no thought of a religious element—as when we say that a certain athletic team didn't have as much talent but that it won because of its "indomitable spirit." We've put it on our license plates in the state of Kentucky, where I now live: an image of a beautiful horse with the phrase, "unbridled spirit." We're looking for the kind of spirit that wins ball games, invigorates people, and that makes for victorious living—not poverty.

It's all the more remarkable that Jesus gave such a rule of happiness to a body of people in the first-century Jewish world. The Jews were living in enforced humility—and enforced humility is humiliation. Humility is a virtue to be sought; humiliation is a condition imposed on us by life or by someone else, and therefore to be escaped. The prevailing power in the first-century world to which Jesus first addressed the Sermon on the Mount was the Roman government. Rome had almost complete power over the lives of its subject peoples. Not only could the Romans tax without restraint or explanation, they could place any number of other indignities upon the people. For instance, a Roman soldier could force any passing Jew—or any other of the subservient peoples—to carry his military pack for a mile simply by laying his spear on a man's shoulder. The Jews were a subject people. On the surface, they were indeed "poor in spirit," with poverty they had never chosen. By contrast the Romans must have been the success story of their day, the ideal to be imitated, and they were anything but "poor in spirit." In such an atmosphere as that, Jesus sang a song of joy about the blessings of humiliation. This, then, is the first of the Beatitudes, the place where they begin. "How happy are the poor in spirit!" The late Dr. George Buttrick said that this Beatitude was "the root from which the others grew."[1] It is no accident that it is the first, because we aren't likely to gain any other of life's virtues unless we begin here. And the promise that Jesus offered in connection with this Beatitude is significant: it is those who are "poor in spirit" who will gain the kingdom of heaven. The succeeding Beatitudes promise a variety of singular blessings, but there's a sense in which "kingdom of heaven" summarizes the whole lot. Get this and you get it all—or, at the least, you've opened the door for all the other benefits. We can't go far toward building a really worthwhile character without encountering the issue of humility—a willing acceptance of our need—which is implied in poverty of spirit.

True humility is so hard to come by. Jewish people tell a wonderful story about a rabbi, a cantor, and a synagogue janitor who were preparing for the Day of Atonement. A true quality of self-abasement is necessary for proper observance of such a holy day. The rabbi beat his breast and said, "I am nothing. I am nothing." Likewise, the cantor beat his breast, crying, "I am nothing. I am nothing." Then the synagogue caretaker, in his soiled, worn clothing, beat his breast and said, "I am nothing. I am nothing." At which point the cantor said to the rabbi, "Look who thinks he's nothing." So subtle is human pride, so elusive a heart that hopes to be poor in spirit.

Eugene Peterson points out the close relationship in the Hebrew language between the word for *poor* and the word for *humble*. He explains that while *poor* designates a socio-economic state, and *humble* a moral-spiritual condition, "What they have in common is nonpossesiveness." This may be by circumstance or by choice, but in either event the person is not in control.[2]

Well, clearly, that's not the way you and I like it. Whether the issue is our finances or any other phase of our lives, we hate to lose control. Indeed, I suggest that being out of control is perhaps the most frustrating and demeaning part of economic poverty. Political theorists remind us that we have only begun to give people their liberty if we give them the right to vote—because if they remain poor, they are still in so many ways subjected people.

How, then, can this Beatitude suggest that being poor—even poor in spirit—is a way of happiness? Jesus' parable of the Pharisee and the tax collector at prayer seems almost like a case study in this Beatitude. You remember it. Two men go to the temple to pray, a Pharisee and a tax collector—a person who in those days made his fortune by dishonest finagling. The Pharisee stands by himself and thanks God that he is "not like other people: thieves, rogues, adulterers, or even like this tax collector." The tax collector, by contrast, dares not even to look upward but beating his breast cries out, "God, be merciful to me, a sinner!" Jesus concludes the story by saying that the tax collector returned home "justified rather than the other" (Luke 18:9-14).

Luke tells us, in introducing the parable, that it is directed against those "who trusted in themselves that they were righteous and regarded others with contempt" (Luke 18:9). Those who trust in the righteousness they see in themselves obviously do not think themselves poor in spirit. Indeed, they feel so rich in righteousness that they have contempt for others. In the process they miss the kingdom of heaven.

But how is it exactly that the poor in spirit have a prior claim—as Jesus sees it—on the kingdom of heaven? This seems contrary to any kingdom we've ever heard of. And especially when it's a heavenly kingdom we have in mind:

surely a kingdom of *heaven* would require its citizens to have extraordinary spiritual riches. Isn't this, after all, what heaven is all about? If Jesus had said that those who are poor in household silver, stock holdings, and property would gain the kingdom of heaven, we could understand it. We might not like it, and we might try to reason around it, but at least we'd see the logic. But poor in *spirit?* Logic seems to insist that the one sure requisite for the kingdom of heaven would be *riches* of spirit.

Well, ponder for a moment how both John the Baptist and Jesus preached about the kingdom of heaven (Matthew 3:1-2; 4:17). They announced the kingdom with a call to repentance. And what is repentance after all but a declaration of poverty? When we repent we tell God that what we have been doing is wrong—that our conduct is bankrupt.

This is a very inelegant way to enter the kingdom. It seems only reasonable that we would approach this kingdom, or any kingdom, with our best qualifications—our letters of reference, our family line, or our SAT scores. And if it's the kingdom of heaven we're seeking, we expect that we will be asked how many good deeds we've done, how much money we've given to the church, or how faithful we are in prayer, study of the Scriptures, and church attendance. Instead, Jesus indicates, the key to entry is our confession of spiritual bankruptcy. In the language of a hymn, "Nothing in my hand I bring, simply to thy cross I cling."

Come to think of it, that's our attitude—at least in the language of our rituals—when we come to the table of Holy Communion. In the ritual I know best the invitation is extended to those who, among other things, "earnestly repent of their sin." And since this is the way, the invitation continues, "Therefore, let us confess our sin before God and one another."[3] And even as I write this, I'm struck by something that somehow hasn't gotten to me before. Not only am I to confess to God that I'm bankrupt—I am also asked to confess this before "one another." Now that's getting about as humbling as life can be.

But when we think about all of this for a moment, we see that this Beatitude has a logic of its own, and a very substantial logic at that. Suppose the Beatitude ran like this: "Blessed are the poor in knowledge, for they shall become learned." Of course! Because the first step in learning is to confess that we don't know everything. Come to think of it, this is one of the reasons small children learn so much faster than adults: they aren't encumbered with the idea that their ignorance is demeaning. So children at a certain age ask "why" endlessly. They aren't embarrassed that they don't know (though they sometimes frustrate us when we have to acknowledge that *we* don't know).

Some of us have had to return to this childhood level of helplessness in adult life with the dominance of the electronic age. My natural aptitude for using a computer, and more recently a cell phone, was almost nonexistent. I had to confess my poverty. Not once, but repeatedly. This experience has been quite good for my soul. Book learning has always come rather easily for me. I was not often embarrassed in the classroom. But when I run into a problem with one of these postmodern devices, I am reduced to kindergarten level.

Or to make the point in another way—and one closer to the issue of poverty of spirit—consider Alcoholics Anonymous. This organization has helped literally millions of addicted persons, but they begin with a simple rule: they can't do a thing for the alcoholic until that person confesses that he or she is an alcoholic and is helpless.

And so it is with all of us. In order to gain eternal life we have to confess that we have no way to buy it. As long as we think we can somehow make it on our own unaided merit, we are too "rich"—like the Pharisee in Jesus' parable—to gain the kingdom. God's kingdom is for those who recognize that they are poor. Nor does the problem cease to exist once we have accepted God's offer of grace, because continuing growth in faith comes by the same pattern of holy poverty. I think that the reason many of us settle in the lowlands of faith is because we cease to feel our need. By contrast, the more saintly we become, the more we sense our poverty—because the closer we draw to our Lord Christ, the more clearly we see what we ought to be, and how far we are from reaching that goal.

But it's so hard to admit our poverty! We do almost anything to avoid such a confrontation. Psychologist Henry Link noted that we often seek to change the social order or others instead of confessing our own need. We'll say almost anything before we'll say, "I'm *poor*. I need help." Even when we confess our poverty we like to add a disclaimer: "I've sinned, but who hasn't?" Or, "I know I'm not perfect, but, after all, who is?"

And of course such reasoning is altogether beside the point. All that really matters for all of us is that we must admit our own poverty, because only then are we on our way to wealth. And until we confess that we are poor, nothing basic can be done for us. The poor in spirit are blessed because in matters of the Spirit, only the poor *get* it. The rest of us wander about in our spiritual rags, thinking we're really quite adequately dressed.

So here, believe it or not, is where the happy way begins: in poverty. Happy are the ignorant, for they shall learn. Happy are those who confess they are ill, because then their doctor can help them. Happy are the weak, because someone else can lend them strength. And happy—how happy!—are the poor in spirit, because they shall enter the kingdom of heaven.

How else did you think any mortal would get into such an immortal place?

CHAPTER *4*

The Happy Mourners

> Blessed are those who mourn, for they will be comforted.

Read Matthew 5:4.

Blessed are those who are grieved over their sins, + those who bear + shore the grief of others.

*A*t the turn of the eighteenth century, the court chaplain to King Louis XIV was Massillon, one of the great preachers of all time. Massillon was an honest and courageous man as well as an admirable scholar. Where persons of lesser character might have catered to the king, Massillon tried always to speak the truth.

Thus on an occasion when he preached to the king about the Beatitude we are about to discuss, "Blessed are they that mourn," Massillon said, "If the world addressed your majesty from this place, the world would not say, 'Blessed are they that mourn,' but 'Blessed is the prince who has never fought but to conquer; who has filled the universe with his name; who through the whole course of a long and flourishing reign enjoys in splendor all that people admire. . . .' But, sire," he continued, "the language of the gospel is not the language of the world."

Indeed it is not. And if that was a problem for a chaplain to the king in the eighteenth century, it is a problem in our time for one who speaks to the general populace. Not only do we live in a time when millions enjoy a lifestyle that King Louis might well envy, palace or not; more than that, we belong to the feel-good age. Even a king in Louis's century was compelled to live intimately with realities that called for mourning, but, except for the television screen, our culture holds death at a distance, provides quick relief for many natural pains, and makes palliatives of one sort or another in reach of almost everyone. Compared to our predecessor generations on this planet, we are a comfortable people, or at the least, people who have some measure of comfort and who usually seek it. And for that matter, why not? If a person despises comfort and seeks pain, we may rightly ask what's wrong with that person.

So of course we're not ready for our Lord when he tells us, in the Sermon on the Mount, "Happy are the mourners!" We know better. Mourning is something to be avoided if at all possible. And if it proves to be inescapable, it is to be endured with stoic courage. We certainly don't expect to find happiness in the place of mourning. In truth, the idea seems almost improper. Perhaps when you saw the title of this chapter you were offended or at least made uneasy. "The Happy Mourner"? The contradiction in terms is so pronounced as to be in bad taste.

No doubt about it, we don't believe in mourning as a way to joy or as a way of life to be sought after. The late J. B. Phillips said that if we humans were to write this Beatitude to reflect life as we see it, we would have it say, "Blessed are the hard-boiled: for they never let life hurt them."[1] I'm afraid that's the Beatitude for a good share of our contemporaries; the only question, perhaps, is the degree to which even earnest Christians sometimes buy into it, consciously or unconsciously. Most of us have been taught to keep a tough exterior and to be careful lest we be unnecessarily open to emotional pain.

So what do we make, then, of Jesus' saying, "Happy those who mourn: they shall be comforted" (JB)? The New

Testament uses an especially powerful word for *mourn*—the strongest available in the Greek language. It is the word that is used to describe mourning for the dead, or the passionate lament for someone who was deeply loved. So, too, the word for *comfort* is a strong one. In the Greek of the New Testament it means "call to the side of." Thus the comfort of which this word speaks is that of someone who has been called to our side in the midst of our need. We don't often stop to think of it, but our English word for comfort is itself a strong word. Its basic root, *fortis*, is the Latin word for *strength.* That is, when someone comforts us they are, quite literally, coming to us with strength. Because of the way we often use the word *comfort*, we're likely to think of it as a quite soft, cuddly word (as in *comfortable*), but in its root form this word conveys the picture of someone coming to us with a transfusion of strength.

But before we go further, let's deal with a natural sentimentality that is likely to influence our thinking in this whole matter. Sorrow itself isn't necessarily good; not by any means. We're right in trying to avoid it. We sometimes say that someone has died of a broken heart, or that because of extreme sorrow someone has lost the will to live. These phrases—like many of our common expressions—contain their own measure of truth. Of itself, left unredeemed, sorrow is an enemy in the journey of life. So how is it, then, that Jesus promised those who mourn that they have reason to be happy, since comfort is coming their way? What did our Lord mean by such a statement?

Let me begin my answer from the "back side"—that is, from an angle that we don't often have in the forefront of our thinking. Specifically, I submit that one thing Jesus may have had in mind is the attitude of sorrow for our sins. I doubt that many of us, in contemplating this Beatitude, have associated it with mourning over the sins we have committed. We think of mourning in connection with some grief or pain that has come our way. And I'll get to that in time (though perhaps not as quickly as you'd like). But let's deal first with what may well have been paramount in Jesus' mind.

Remember that Jesus began his ministry with the same message as John the Baptist: "Repent!" The basic quality of repentance is a sense of profound sorrow for the wrong we have done, along with a passion to turn life in a different direction. Which is to say, there are some things very worth mourning about; and if that is so, mourning is a state of mind worth seeking on its own merit. Consider, also, that this Beatitude follows hard on the heels of "Blessed are the poor in spirit." Those who recognize that they are poor in spirit demonstrate their poverty—their holy humility—by a godly sorrow for their sins, for their failure to live up to God's purpose in their lives.

Our spiritual ancestors on the American frontier had a strange and wonderful practice. In their revival meetings they maintained a seat or a pew near the pulpit, at the very front of the meetinghouse, for those who were especially concerned about the condition of their souls. They called this pew "the mourner's bench," to acknowledge that the people who sat there were distressed over the evil and the shortcoming in their lives. So distressed, in fact, that they would sit in a place where the community of worshipers could identify them as sinners and could know that they were seeking relief. I ask myself how often I have been so unhappy over the wrongs I have done that I would station myself on a mourner's bench, thus making public declaration of my need. Perhaps if we did so we might feel a comfort greater than we can imagine. But believe me, this mourner's bench would be a hard sell in our feel-good culture!

John Wesley, the father of the Methodist movement, felt that this Beatitude was primarily concerned with repentance. He said that those who wished to receive the blessings of God's comfort would need to mourn "either for their own sins, or for other men's," and be "steadily and habitually serious" in this concern. Wesley knew from experience, of course, for he had undergone great anguish over his own spiritual shortcomings. And—thank God!—he also knew that comfort comes to those who mourn for their sins.

When we mourn for our sins, we gain a new sensitivity to the rights and feelings of others. Notice that we are speaking of mourning for *sins*, not for the consequences which we fear may come upon us because of our sins. When we have such a concern for the harm our sins may do to some other human being and to the heart and purposes of God, our mourning gets a quality that is wondrous to observe. Without it, we see what wrongs others have done to us or how we have suffered some injustice; but when the sorrow of sin comes to us, we are impressed instead with the pain others are experiencing. In some instances this may lead even to our making restitution for the harm we've done. This is good sorrow, and it is the kind of mourning that brings comfort, just as Jesus promised.

There's no doubt about it: After we have repented of our sins before God and have, if possible and necessary, made things right with some other person, we experience a very deep and fulfilling joy. Some gospel songs of another generation spoke often about the joy of sins forgiven. A postmodern might think, from studying such hymns, that our ancestors were obsessed with a sense of guilt. Perhaps the opposite was true: they had found a way to be done with guilt. Our culture is more likely, on the one hand, to confront guilt with professional aid via a psychiatrist or a counselor; or on the other hand, through abusing drugs or alcohol—which is, of course, an exacerbating of the problem rather than dealing with it. When you contrast the person who evades dealing with sins with the one who—in healthy fashion—mourns for them, you begin to see one important aspect of what Jesus meant when he said, "Happy are those who mourn, for they shall be comforted." Godly mourning makes for strength, the kind of profound, inner strength that makes great human beings.

But there's more to Jesus' promise than this. Happy, too, is that person who *mourns for others.* We belong to a world where pain is all around us. On the day you or I go whistling down the street, glad for sunshine and achievement, the person we pass may be weeping within because of the illness of spouse or child, or the agony of rejection. While we're attending a party celebrating a promotion, someone in our neighborhood is in dull despair over the treadmill quality of his or her career. On the Saturday of one person's wedding reception, another is coping with rejection. In a world like ours, we need people who are willing to hurt for the pain of others.

We hear sometimes of a person who on the field of battle throws his own body on an explosive to protect the lives of others in his company. Such heroism is almost beyond imagination, and not many of us will ever have opportunity to give ourselves so unselfishly. But all of us have opportunities of another, less dramatic kind. We can help break the impact of some missile of pain, absorbing some of the pain into our own persons. Charles Williams, the British novelist who was a close friend and literary associate of C. S. Lewis, describes such a character, Stanhope, in his novel, *Descent into Hell.* Stanhope offers to take the burden from a young woman in distress; but he insists that she must let him have it—so that, like a person who volunteers to carry our parcels, we don't try then to carry the parcels ourselves. I have known several instances where people entered into my time of need with such a quality of caring that I left their presence feeling that they had quite literally carried away some of my pain.

Since the cost of such mourning is so great, most of us are cautious about involving ourselves. We may, in fact, run from the person in trouble. The self-centered say, "I have troubles enough of my own." Others of more tender sensibilities explain, "I never know what to say." I understand this feeling; I've had it often myself. But in truth, this isn't a major shortcoming. Most people in hard places of life don't so much need words of counsel as they do a hand of affection and strength, or a listening ear.

But it's not easy to be a listening ear—the kind of listener, that is, who absorbs the pain of the speaker—or a hand of affection and strength. So we generally avoid such relationships. This is unfortunate, because if we will not allow our hearts to be broken by the pain of others, we make our own lives smaller. Here is the wisdom of Jesus' rule: when we mourn for the sorrows of others, we not only bring comfort to them but also—miraculously it sometimes seems—to ourselves.

That's why a doctor, a minister, or a psychiatrist will sometimes encourage a newly bereaved person to become involved in some work of mercy. If persons in such circumstances will get out of themselves enough to feel the pain and need of someone else, they will diminish their own grief. There's no better way to find comfort for one's own soul than to take upon ourselves the burden of some other person. In the process of relieving another, we are ourselves relieved. "How happy are those who mourn for the pain of others, for in bringing comfort they gain comfort."

But it's clear that I must say still another word. There can be blessing in mourning even when the mourning is from our own sorrows. When I first began pondering this Beatitude, I faced a problem. I could see well enough that the person who was mourning needed comfort—indeed, comfort is precisely what one needs at such a time. But this gave no special credibility to the mourning itself. Why not get life's strength without ever facing the agony of sorrow? It seemed to me that this "comfort" that sorrow might bring is something most of us would be glad enough to get along without.

So we have to grasp the fact of it, the hard but wonderful

fact. There are some qualities in life that cannot be had without the price of suffering. Especially, there are some qualities of character that can be bought in only this way. "When things go well," William Barclay (a man who knew a great deal about suffering) wrote, "it is possible to live for years on the surface of things; but when sorrow comes a [person] is driven to the deep things of life, and, if he [or she] accepts it aright, a new strength and beauty enter into his [or her] soul."[2]

I hardly need to give examples, because most of us have several of our own. Dr. Ralph W. Sockman—another person who knew deep personal pain—said that a man may spend his time with sporting companions and professional associates when life is easy, and his friendships will remain at a superficial level. But when a hard place comes, he wants something deeper than the hail-fellow-well-met; he wants a friendship with depth and quality. One may paint pretty little pictures when life is easy, but after there has been hurt inside, we handle our brush with new power and intensity, and we discover the beauty that can come only with the delicate shadings of shadows.

Psychologist Henry Link wrote a generation ago, "All the material advantages of our civilization conspire to make our lives easier and our characters weaker." He felt that parents often do their children "irreparable harm" by protecting them from all test and responsibility. If he could make only one recommendation for our American educational system, Dr. Link said, it would be that every young person spend a year sometime between eighteen and twenty-one working at public physical labor.[3] Some might see it as inflicted physical hardship; in truth, the discipline of the hardship would prove to be a blessing.

Often when I look at pictures of babies in the early weeks of life, when so many pictures are taken, I entertain a rather heretical idea. Tiny infants pretty much look alike—with the exception, of course, of your children or grandchildren. It's the experience of living, including especially the tests of life, that brings quality and character into our faces, until at last we get the face we've earned. So isn't it strange that we take so many pictures when our faces are unformed, so to speak, and so few after our experiences have written their story into our features? And is there anything more beautiful than that person who has grown old with such dignity and character that we see in them an unconscious holiness?

How happy are those who mourn, for they shall be made strong: *comforted.* As Massillon said to Louis XIV, this is not the language of the world. But of course that shouldn't surprise us, because the secular culture obviously doesn't know much about happiness. It is expert in activities and pursuits that mask pain or that provide temporary escape, but not in the deep happiness that is independent of circumstances.

CHAPTER **5**

The Meek Laugh Best

Blessed are the meek, for they will inherit the Earth!

Read Matthew 5:5.

The Sermon on the Mount has been called an ethical teaching for heroes. As I review the Beatitudes, I agree readily. Suffering persecution for goodness' sake is certainly beyond the reach of spiritual weaklings. And there's nothing soft about being a peacemaker, either; in fact, it can be hard, dangerous work. As for purity, it looks easy only to those who haven't seriously tried it.

But as for "happy are the meek," that's something else again. It takes quite an imagination to see heroism in meekness. The phrase that first comes to my mind when I hear the word *meek* is "meek as a lamb." That may work for a pretty pastoral scene, but it doesn't evoke images of heroism. Or I think of that obsequious Charles Dickens character, Uriah Heep, who traded in mock meekness. Or that strangely loveable even if pathetic character, the comic strip personality of a generation ago, Casper Milquetoast; he didn't need a shadow to frighten him, his shadows were built in.

So how can Jesus say, "Happy are the meek"? It's a bit like

saying, "Happy are the downtrodden," or the "subjugated"—except that the downtrodden and the subjugated may still have a protest in their soul, so that no matter what their condition, they retain some inner dignity. But the *meek?* Not only are they afflicted and downtrodden, they seem to embrace such a condition. I see no heroism here.

And that's only the beginning of the problem with this Beatitude. See what Jesus promised to the meek: *they shall inherit the earth.* You and I know better. The meek can't even inherit the right-of-way at a traffic intersection or a place in the grocery checkout line. If Jesus had said that the meek will inherit *heaven,* we would understand the promise. We know that the meek ought to get something someday, and since it's clear they'll never get anything on this earth, it's nice to think God will provide them with compensation in the world to come. But bless you, this Beatitude makes no reference to the world to come; it promises reward on this earth. When Jesus says something as outrageous as the meek inheriting the earth, we figure that Jesus just didn't know the world you and I live in. This earth is the last thing the meek will inherit, unless we're talking about some burnt-over portion that the rest of the populace (those real go-getters) have forsaken.

Obviously, this Beatitude runs counter to almost everything we believe and practice in daily life. We say, "You have to fight for your rights." Jesus answers, "The meek shall inherit the earth." History seems built on the theme of the survival of the fittest, and the meek don't fulfill that description. We think happiness is to be found in the display of power; Jesus taught that happiness is found in the restraint of whatever power we may have.

What does it mean to be meek? Dictionaries define meekness as "mild of temper" or "patient under injuries." But I want to lead us beyond dictionary definitions because these definitions aren't big enough to handle the word that appears in the Bible; that is, the languages in which the Bible was originally written and the contexts of the biblical understanding.

Let's begin by looking at some definitions in action: that is, people who are specifically described as being meek. The Bible uses the word for two persons in particular, Moses and Jesus.

The Bible says of Moses that he was "very meek, above all the men which were upon the face of the earth" (Numbers 12:3 KJV). Yet Moses was anything but a Casper Milquetoast. He wasn't weak, and he wasn't without a temper, and at times he wasn't even particularly patient. He was a person of such charismatic personality that he could unite a group of dispirited slaves into a nation, then lead them for forty years through a trackless wilderness. He dared to challenge the most powerful ruler of his day in repeated confrontations, and in his devotion to his people he even argued with God. I know of few personalities in all of human history—indeed, in all of literature—who demonstrated more sheer strength and fierce courage, yet the Scriptures describe him as the meekest of men. Pretty clearly, the Bible definition of meekness is different from our popular image of the word.

The Bible also uses the word *meek* in describing Jesus. Those who think of Jesus with the hymn phrase, "gentle Jesus, meek and mild," might feel that the usual definition of meekness applies. But his meekness, too, was of a startling kind. Again and again Jesus stood up to the challenge of enemies, both individuals and hostile crowds. When he returned to his hometown, Nazareth, he was so forthright in talking with the people that they sought to push him off a precipice, but he walked calmly through the crowd, untouched. There's nothing weak about that! Jesus endured sham trials with unshakeable dignity, and suffered physical abuse from soldiers without losing control of his emotions. Finally, in the hour of his crucifixion he was so strong that he could pray for his enemies; in the last hour of his dying his strength evoked the admiration of a tough-minded Roman centurion, a man whose job compelled him daily to

traffic in courage. Gordon Powell says that there was something about Jesus' meekness "that frightened some people,
especially those who were morally weak or positively evil."
Powell then observes that when Jesus talked about meekness, he was talking about something that requires very
great strength; he was speaking of self-control.[1]

So let's come back to the New Testament word for
meek—a quite special Greek word, the word *praus*. Aristotle
defined every virtue as the mean between two extremes. He
described this word, *praus*, as the proper ground between
excessive anger and excessive angerlessness. William
Barclay therefore suggests that this Beatitude could be
translated, "Blessed is the [person] who is always angry at
the right time, and never angry at the wrong time."[2]

That's a pretty big assignment, isn't it? In the first place,
most of us probably feel that anger is always bad, but this
isn't so. Our world needs the right kind of anger—the
kind of anger that is carefully channeled to curing the
world's ills. A good teacher is angry about ignorance; a
physician is angry about illness; a true diplomat is angry
about war; a growing Christian is angry about sin. I venture that every great cause, every great human gain, would
die if it were not for people who have gotten angry with
things as they are.

But on the other hand, misused anger is the most
destructive of powers. And that's where meekness comes in.
The meek person is always angry at the right time, and
never angry at the wrong time.

Let me give you another insight from the way the Greeks
used this word in the first century. In their training of animals, this word *praus* was used to describe an animal that
had been domesticated, a creature of great power, but with
the power brought under control. As one writer has sug-
gested, if you want to understand this concept of meekness,
you should picture a majestic draft horse—a great
Clydesdale, for example—muscles rippling, but subject to

the reins and to its training. This is meekness as Jesus is using the word. As Ralph Sockman once said, it takes strength to be gentle. A weak person can't be gentle. Uncertain and inadequate, perhaps, but not gentle. A meek person, therefore, is not a weak person but a very, very strong one. So strong, in fact, that he or she is able to hold strength under control, so that the strength is used for right purposes.

So the poet Mary Karr has it right when she sees "meek" defined in "a great stallion at full gallop" that will halt at the master's voice.[3] I saw "meek" when I stood one day at the site of a great dam. Millions of tons of water were stored behind the wall, water more quiet than a languid stream. But when those tons of water are directed to their purpose, they generate massive electrical power. Massive power, under control, ready to fulfill a purpose.

So our usual perceptions miss this word badly. We see a Uriah Heep character and think that this is meekness, while in truth it is meanness, a sniveling, obsequious quality. We caricature meekness with a Casper Milquetoast, which is a cowardly cover for insecurity, the farthest remove from "a stallion at full gallop."

The secret of meekness, therefore, is not to have nothing. Rather, it is to have power, resources, and strength, yet not be influenced by them or made arrogant by their potential. The meek person doesn't have to "claim his rights," because he or she fully possesses those rights. It's when we don't know our power that we have to throw our weight around, have to assert ourselves, in order to convince ourselves that we're in control. The meek don't have to prove themselves to themselves.

Let me put it in very simple terms. Who is stronger, the person who strikes back or the one who doesn't need to? If a small child hits a man, the man doesn't hit him back (unless, of course, the man is immature). The man has the power to do what he wants with the child, but he has an even greater power, the strength to hold his superiority under control.

We see our point in the bully. A bully is a bully precisely because he or she doesn't have the strength to be anything else. A bully is never really a strong person; the bully suffers the inestimable weakness of needing to prove that he's tough. And incidentally, bullies are not limited to the world of fists and weapons; bullies are also to be found among managers, executives, and even teachers and preachers, if they use their tongues and some measure of their intelligence to humiliate or control others. The meek person doesn't have to be a bully. The meek know who they are, so they have little to prove. They have the inner strength to control their power.

But you're still wondering about the way Jesus concluded this Beatitude: the meek shall "inherit the earth." Perhaps you've seen enough dictators, large and small, that you're not at all sure Jesus knew what he was talking about—or at the least, that Jesus must have had in mind a perfect world, not this one. So let me tell you how the meek inherit the earth.

For one thing, they inherit friends. Aggressive people insist on their own way, demand their rights in relationships, dominate conversations—and lose friends. The meek restrain themselves, listen at least as much as they speak, are able to recognize when the other person is right, and enjoy letting someone else's ego flourish—and in the process, they inherit friends.

The meek inherit peace of mind. People who constantly demand their rights rarely get much satisfaction, even when they win. Have you ever stood on the edge of an argument in a place of business and watched the mood of the angry person who "wins"? Does that person walk away smiling? Rarely. Instead, the "winner" goes out the door still muttering, muttering, muttering. He or she wins everything but happiness. How happy are the meek, for they inherit peace of mind.

And of course the meek inherit knowledge; yes, and more than that, they inherit wisdom. The great Lord Kelvin left his mark in so many areas of applied science, but his students remembered him best for his meekness and humility. George Washington Carver worked nothing short of miracles in his simple laboratory, but he began each day's work with meekness, bowing his head before God to seek strength. And while I am thinking of meekness primarily in its application as a Christian virtue, its basic truth is all around us. Thomas Huxley, the premier nineteenth century British scientist, once wrote Charles Kingsley that the rule of science was to "sit down before the facts as a little child," because the only way to learn was to "be prepared to give up every preconceived notion," and to be led to whatever end nature might lead one to. There's meekness in that posture, isn't there?

And especially, the meek inherit their own abilities. I remember Dr. Ralph Sockman as a person who refused to be impressed with his own achievements or with the endless accolades that came his way, so I find it easy to believe him when he wrote, "the meek get more values out of themselves because their passions are under control and not ever beating against the bars, using up energy which might be otherwise used."[4] Those who try to impress people never make full use of their personalities, because their personalities are obscured by self-concern. Persons who want to be noticed are rarely as attractive as they could be because their natural attractiveness is distorted by artificiality. But the meek inherit their own abilities. They get themselves off their hands, and thus are freer to use the gifts God has given them.

Does it occur to you that, in a wonderful sense, the meek—as Jesus described them—are a wonderfully *confident* people? They know who they are, and are sure enough of their powers that they don't need to parade those powers. They have no compulsion to demonstrate their strength because they have brought their strength under the control of God's spirit of love.

How *happy* are the meek, for they shall inherit the earth! Surely this is one of the most practical pieces of advice to be found anywhere. And in many ways it is as earthy and earthly as the reward it promises, while at the same time it is profoundly spiritual. Because the persons who are free enough of themselves to be meek are already partaking of the life of God's kingdom.

I wonder if someone is wishing just now that they could ask this author if he has himself achieved this quality of meekness. In truth, I'm still working on it. I have some small sense of how beautiful true meekness is, so I know it's worth pursuing—and I also realize that it isn't easily attained because it is so contrary to our normal human nature. If we're to be meek, we'll need help from outside ourselves. Dr. Sockman was right when he said that the meekness that Jesus commanded is a matter of being *God-mastered.* We win mastery over ourselves by giving mastery over to God.

I've been fortunate over the years of my life to have known a fair number of political personalities, farmers, Hall of Fame athletes, deliverymen, millionaires, international scholars, table servers, and public personalities, and it's been interesting to see those who have inherited the earth and those who are still trying to stake a claim. I've found that it has little to do with position, power, or money, and that it has almost everything to do with what is inside the person. Those who are at peace with God and with themselves about their true worth inherit the earth, and they show it by the disciplined way they use the power they possess.

And they tend to laugh rather easily. After all, when you're meek, and you're inheriting the earth, there's plenty to laugh about.

CHAPTER

6

The Hunger Road to Happiness

" Blessed are those who hunger +
thirst for rightousness , for they
will be filled."

Read Matthew 5:6.

The Beatitude we're about to discuss has a double fault. It begins with something we don't understand and ends at a place we don't necessarily want to go. We want to be happy, of course. As I've mentioned before, Americans think they have a right to happiness or at least, the right to pursue it—because this right is written into their basic political document. But when America's founders put this "right" into a political statement they were only declaring formally what we humans have always thought is our right. I suppose, in fact, that this is a key element in the story of the Garden of Eden: when the serpent presented Adam and Eve with an offer of more happiness than they were currently enjoying, they were quick to buy into the deal.

So we're all for happiness and always have been. But when a Beatitude suggests that *righteousness* is a factor in happiness, most of us happiness-shoppers move on to another department. And when we're assured that our quest for righteousness will be satisfied, we find it hard to get excited since righteousness doesn't seem to be our major craving—especially when we're told that we'll have to hunger and thirst to get this benefit that we're not even sure we want. Well, you get the point. This Beatitude is a hard sell.

Let's begin, however, with a bit of obvious logic. When we're told that if we "hunger and thirst" we'll be satisfied, we have something that from one point of view seems close to a truism—namely, that desire is essential to satisfaction. It is through hunger that we come to happiness. Although hunger itself (or longing, to put the concept in a different form) may entail a great deal of pain, it is through this discomfort that satisfaction comes. The sick person, told to eat in order to speed up recovery, answers, "But I just don't have an appetite." The patient needs the discomfort of hunger in order to enjoy the satisfaction that eating will bring.

This rule applies in all areas of life. As a teacher, I love those students who hunger for knowledge. The teacher who worked with the young Paderewski had an educator's paradise; we'd all love to have a student who hungered so much for excellence that he would practice eighteen hours a day! By contrast, no teaching assignment is as difficult as the student with no appetite, no desire to learn. Satisfaction begins with hunger; longing is essential to fulfillment.

But most of us have a problem with the figure of speech Jesus used—hungering and thirsting—because most of us have never really been hungry for food. Not in our adult lives, at any rate. Babies understand hunger, because instinctively they know that if they don't get food they will die. At regular intervals, therefore, a baby cries desperately; and any of us who have been around an infant have seen the satisfaction that comes when food is supplied.

Not many of us, however, experience such hunger in our adult lives. That's why we find it so difficult to empathize with stories of starvation from other parts of the world. In truth, I suspect that the food and entertainment publications and television programs are meant to stimulate hunger in people who are already satiated. The medieval peasant who returned from the fields at the end of the day was so hungry that bread, soup, and fruit—basic items, with little or no adornment—were a feast. Some of us have to develop a facsimile hunger by going to a restaurant that has "atmosphere," with a menu whose items are fortified by exotic phrases. All of this to make us *hunger*, so that when the meal is over we will be *satisfied*.

A large share of the persons who first heard Jesus teach understood hunger—as do vast numbers in our present world. So many of the common people in the first century world were never too far from starvation. That's why the Old Testament law required that an employer pay wages to his workers each evening, because the poor existed on a day-to-day basis. If the employer made his workers wait a day for their salaries, the worker and his family might well go hungry. As for water, in that world and climate a well or a cistern was literally a matter of life and death.

But even if the phrase "hunger and thirst" doesn't have the same physical impact on us as it had on the people of Jesus' day or on people in those places where life is so marginal, it still describes a feeling that all of us experience in particular areas of life. We know what it means through our experience with other hungers and thirsts—matters emotional, social, sexual, aesthetic, and intellectual.

But this brings us back to the issue from which I detoured a few minutes ago. How many of us have ever thought of hungering for *righteousness?* Honestly, righteousness usually doesn't excite us that much. It seems that most people can take it or leave it, and generally they choose to leave it. Some people, in fact, seem to run from any prospect of righteousness. Not many of us concentrate the very real longings of our souls toward righteousness.

Perhaps part of the problem in our thinking, however,

lies in our definition of righteousness. For one thing, we think instinctively of several other worthy qualities that seem more important than righteousness. Love, for instance. A perennially popular song says that "what the world needs now is love, sweet love." Most people will buy into that. Why not, then, hunger for love rather than righteousness? Or with continuing strife in several parts of the world, I suspect that many feel Jesus might better have urged us to hunger and thirst for peace. And then again, there's faith. Jesus said that with proper faith we can move mountains. As we think of the mountains of anguish, loneliness, fear, hatred, hunger, and other forms of human tragedy, if we could unleash faith to move those mountains—well, that would be something to hunger and thirst for!

Yet Jesus recommended a passionate hunger for *righteousness*. What did he have in mind?

One thing is clear. Jesus was speaking of righteousness quite beyond our usual, perhaps rather comfortable, definitions. Just a little farther along in this Sermon on the Mount, Jesus warned that our righteousness must exceed that of the scribes and Pharisees or we "will never enter the kingdom of heaven" (Matthew 5:20). Most of the folks in Jesus' day saw the scribes and Pharisees as the exemplars of righteousness. They may not have liked these two groups, but they looked upon them as the ultimate authorities on what was right and good. But Jesus said, in an almost matter-of-fact way, that he was looking for far more.

So was Jesus speaking of personal righteousness, the saintly longing to be a better, holier human being? Or was he speaking of social righteousness, the kind of goodness that brings justice to all humanity? The different translations of the Bible seem to suggest both possibilities—perhaps reflecting the theological prejudices of the several translators. One translation says, "Happy are those who are hungry and thirsty for true goodness" (JBP). Another says,

"Happy are those whose greatest desire is to do what God requires" (GNT). These translations can easily be seen as emphasizing personal purity and holiness. But another translator says, "Blessed are those who hunger and thirst for justice" (Lamsa), and still another says, "Blessed are those who hunger and thirst for righteousness." These phrases, in turn, sound like a cry for social justice and reform. Which did Jesus have in mind, personal righteousness or pervading social justice?

Or could it just be that our question reveals a problem in our souls? Are we inclined toward one emphasis or another because we find it easier to achieve that particular goal? In truth, is it possible to separate personal and social righteousness? Are they not, really and finally, of one piece? And has our desire to emphasize one over the other prevented our gaining either one?

Here is an instance where we will find help by turning to the Greek, the language in which the New Testament was originally written. I hasten to say that I'm not relying on my own limited knowledge of the Greek; I'm drawing on the scholarship of far more capable persons. Hold with me while I take us into Greek grammar for a moment. In biblical Greek, verbs of *hungering* and *thirsting* are followed by the genitive case, expressed in our language by the preposition *of.* Specifically, these words call for something known as the partitive genitive, which means that if we would translate them literally into the English we would say, "I thirst *for of* water." This would mean to thirst for a drink of water but not for all the water in the tank. But in this Beatitude the New Testament puts "righteousness" in the accusative case instead of the genitive, so that the meaning is that the hunger and thirst is for the whole thing. If you were to say, "I thirst for water," and put it in the accusative case, you would mean, "I thirst for all the water in the container"—or stream, or well, or reservoir; whatever. Thus if we translate this Beatitude literally we would say, "Happy are those who hunger and thirst for *all* of righteousness, *total* righteousness."

This kind of reading is consistent with the whole body of Jesus' call to discipleship. Our Lord said that those who would follow him must "deny themselves and take up their cross," and be ready to "lose their life" for his sake (Matthew 16:24-25).

That is, righteousness is a life-demanding, life-involving thing. It isn't relegated to one phase of life, nor is it something we celebrate during certain seasons; righteousness is a way of life, and a magnificently challenging and fulfilling way.

Our problem, then, is that we don't often thirst for all of righteousness. Instead we thirst for our cause, the needs of our group, or our own sense of need. So of course this attitude infects the religious community as a whole, in a way that shows itself particularly in Protestantism, but that also has its manifestations in Catholicism. There are those, on the one hand, who earnestly and devoutly seek a deep, personal faith. They are drawn to retreats and renewal events; they are admirably faithful in their personal devotional life, in prayer and Bible study. But they may seem almost oblivious to some of the injustices in the world except perhaps to pray about these injustices from time to time.

On the other hand, the church has a substantial number who strive earnestly to bring righteousness—especially as it expresses itself in justice and social concern—to public issues. They are ready for every good cause, often in the forefront of reform and political action. But sometimes these persons seem indifferent to the pursuit of personal faith. They want righteousness for the world, but they are dull to the idea of righteousness in personal habits and conduct. In each case, I'm drawing exaggerated pictures so you will understand my point; but as a matter of fact, sometimes my picture seems tame compared to the displayed facts.

All of which demonstrates dramatically how badly we need to give attention to this Beatitude. "Happy are those who hunger and thirst for *total* righteousness"—the whole, demanding package, the whole wonderful, transforming way of life. You see, most of our righteousness is too fragmentary. We want righteousness where it's convenient, but we aren't too excited about becoming righteous people. And I suspect that this is why we humans so often pervert righteousness into that abominable thing we call self-righteousness. It's very easy, you know, to feel good about yourself if you're seeking only partial righteousness, because partial righteousness is easy to come by. Thus the person whose religion is a matter of reading the Bible rather often and praying can feel satisfied with himself; and so, too, with the person whose morality is exclusively on public issues such as world peace and poverty. But if we seek *total* righteousness—concern for both our private conduct and for the world in which we live, we will be left with little energy to invest in self-righteousness.

But how exactly is satisfaction to be found in this hungering and thirsting for righteousness? Most of us who have sought righteousness learn that we don't necessarily get the righteousness for which we seek, whether it be personal goodness or social justice. Indeed, we learn after a while to brace ourselves for disappointment in our quest. Some feel that they struggle all through life for holiness and righteousness yet never seem to attain it, just as others give a lifetime to some great cause of justice and mercy and never see the battle won. How then can Jesus say, "Happy [are] those who hunger and thirst for what is right; / they shall be satisfied" (JB)?

Always remember this, that the hunger for righteousness is hunger at the *heart* of life. Remember Saint Augustine's classic cry: "Thou hast made us for thyself, and our hearts are restless till they find their rest in thee." This is hunger at the heart of life; not its periphery, not its transient interests, but at the place where the issues and meaning of life are fully spelled out. You see the point, don't you? Most of our hungers seem to concentrate on the marginal and the superficial; as a result, when such hungers are met, we are still left unsatisfied. But the hunger for righteousness is at the center of our being; indeed, at the very heart of who we are and of creation itself. Thus we are dealing with a matter worthy of our God-given humanity. So, then, we find a unique fulfillment in the search itself. The hunger is, in a profound sense, its own reward. As eternal creatures we are energized by our involvement in an eternal pursuit.

Dr. Ralph Sockman put it perfectly. "[We] must have more than enough to live on. [We] must have enough to live *for*."[1] The quest for righteousness brings a lively hunger to life. There is profound reason to get up in the morning, and then to seek rest at night. Life has a *cause*, a purpose: what is *right*. And *all* right—rightness within and rightness without; rightness in our own souls and rightness for the world in which our souls reside. This is far more, you see, than winning a battle with a bad temper, fine as that achievement would be for many of us, and it's more than electing a particular candidate or passing special legislation. This is a glorious seeking after life's holy grail, the rightness of God and God's glory in all of life.

And especially, remember this word of good hope. Jesus did not say, "Blessed are those who become righteous." If he had, few if any of us would ever receive the blessing. But this Beatitude reflects the grace of God: we are judged by our intentions rather than our achievements. It is our hungering and thirsting that win the praise of our Lord, not our accomplishments.

In it all, we have a grand confidence. When we hunger and thirst for righteousness, we have committed ourselves to a cause that "can never be lost or stayed." God and eternity are on our side. The battle may be long; indeed, it is. We may lose frequent skirmishes along the way; I surely have. We may look at the inadequacies of our personal lives and be frustrated or even ashamed, then look at the world in which we have invested our lives and our prayers and feel little ground has been gained. But then we look at our Lord, the Author and Finisher of our faith. And looking, we remember that he is on our side. The battle will be won. It cannot be otherwise.

"How happy are those who hunger and thirst for total, life-encompassing righteousness. They are living at the heart of the matter. They shall be satisfied."

CHAPTER 7

12/03/08

Many Happy Returns

Blessed are the merciful, for they will be shown mercy!

Read Matthew 5:7.

N ow and then a rather typical, popular novel or movie leaves a person with the impact of some memorable scene—one that seems to overpower all else you remember from the story. That's the case with Morton Thompson's novel of almost a generation ago, *Not as a Stranger.* It is the story of a young physician—brilliant and able, but also impatient (as the brilliant and able sometimes are) with the mistakes and limitations of others. In an especially dramatic incident the young doctor goes to the head of the district medical association to accuse an older doctor of malpractice. The head of the association urges the young doctor not to be hasty and not to judge too harshly. But the young man is unmoved. As I recall it, at this point the association head leans across his desk to say, "I am going to suggest this to you—that if you persist in bringing formal charges, then be sure of one thing. Don't ever, as long as you live, make a single mistake."

I don't recall if the director spoke those words by way of threat, to suggest that if the opportunity came he would treat the doctor as unmercifully as the doctor was treating the older colleague, or whether the director spoke in more philosophical terms, inferring that life treats us as we treat others. In either case, the story is to the point of the Beatitude that is before us: "Happy [are] the merciful; / they shall have mercy shown them" (JB). There come times in every life when we need mercy; for that reason most of us are grateful for the latter half of this Beatitude: we hope we will receive mercy when we need it. But, being human, we may not be as attentive to the opening portion of the verse, the one that calls us to the posture of mercy. This is where this Beatitude puts us to the test.

Let me repeat: all of us need mercy at some time or another. Nobody is so perfect in his or her conduct or so free from error, or possessed of so much power that the need for mercy will not on some occasion exist. The soldier needs mercy when he appears before his king, but the king needs mercy when he comes to his surgeon. Mercy is a kind of endless procession, a parade of human frailty. The failing student needs mercy when he stands before his teacher, the teacher needs it when facing an issue with the principal, the principal before the school superintendent, the superintendent at presentations before the school board, and the school board when unhappy parents and taxpayers call. Don't bother with the question, *Who needs mercy?* Ask, rather, *How soon? How often? How much?*

So the words of our Beatitude make wonderfully good sense: "Happy are the merciful, for they shall obtain mercy." Why not assure ourselves of mercy, in sensible anticipation of the time when we'll need it? And the promise tends to be true: merciful people do seem to receive mercy in return. They don't necessarily receive it from the persons to whom they extended it, but it comes. In fact, perhaps the mercy comes more often in a peculiar pattern: we show mercy to some person, who then shows it to another, and the third (or the twentieth) returns mercy to us. But the many happy returns go on, with mercy bringing mercy, on and on and on.

Nor should the interpretation and understanding of what Jesus said be limited to this earth. Thanks be to God, there is a final Judge. We sometimes see instances—are sometimes, in fact, participants in instances—where the merciful don't get their fair share of mercy on this earth. I must qualify this statement, of course, because we're rarely in a position to make accurate appraisals of another person's experience of mercy and reward. Nevertheless, I remind myself of an old saying: all of life's accounts aren't settled in September.

But let me remind us of a story Jesus told about mercy (Matthew 18:21-35). He could well have told it as a warning illustration for the Beatitude we're discussing. A great king was settling accounts with his servants, people whom he had trusted with significant responsibilities. One of them had done poorly, so now he owed the king several million dollars—a debt he couldn't remotely meet. The king decided to foreclose the debt by selling the man and his family into slavery. But when the man appealed, the king released him and forgave his debt.

You would expect that this man would now go out and shower kindness on other people. Instead, irrationally and wickedly, he did just the opposite. When he came upon a fellow servant who owed him a modest debt (something under ten dollars, comparatively speaking), he seized the man by the throat, demanding payment. The man appealed for mercy and time, but his appeal was summarily refused. When news of this shameful incident reached the king, the king called the servant to him. "You wicked slave!" he said. "I forgave you all that debt because you pleaded with me. Should you not have had mercy on your fellow slave?" And the king delivered him to the jailers.

This is one of those stories where we're supposed to laugh even as we get the point. The details of the story are wildly exaggerated, with the comparison between a debt of ten dollars and one of several million. That's the mood the story is trying to get across: that all of us have been forgiven so grandly by God that any debt owed us by another human is so inconsequential as to be, by comparison, ridiculous. We have received mercy in abundance; shouldn't we, therefore, gladly extend it to others? And Jesus concludes with a not-so-funny fact: if we don't show mercy, we can be sure that a day of reckoning will come, whether in this world or the next.

On the one hand, there's consolation in Jesus' story. If it seems to you that someone you know has not received mercy, you can be sure that there is mercy yet to be shown. God, the ultimate source of mercy, will grant mercy to those who have been merciful to others.

But of course there's more to the Beatitude than this. When we speak of mercy and our need of it and our hope that we will receive it, we need to look carefully at the price tag that is attached to mercy. We get mercy by extending mercy. "Blessed are the merciful, for they will receive mercy." We're inclined to speak these words easily, as if we have always extended mercy, and as if mercy were a simple matter. Ralph Sockman observed that we often say that all this world needs is the "simple art of being kind." But he continues, "The trouble is that the art of being kind is not so simple."[1] Obviously not. If it were, the practice of kindness would be much more prevalent; would, indeed, become a way of life for most human beings.

Believe me, mercy is hard work. For one thing, mercy is an emotional investment. The biblical conception of mercy, William Barclay said, means "the ability to get right inside the other person's skin until we can see things with his eyes, think things with his mind, and feel things with his feelings."[2] Between you and me, this is the kind of total involvement that most of the time we can't even imagine—and that when we do imagine it, we're likely to avoid it. It's the kind of involvement that the British novelist, Charles

Williams, describes in his novel *Descent into Hell*, when he speaks of one's literally picking up another person's pain so that it is no longer theirs to carry. When we face the prospect of this kind of involvement, we're less likely to pass judgment on the priest and the Levite (in Jesus' story of the good Samaritan) who chose to pass by on the other side. It's far easier to avoid looking pain in the eye than to invest ourselves in such mercy that we see with the sufferer's eyes and feel with the sufferer's feelings. Mercy involves more than a financial contribution, essential as that is, and more even than a note or a passing visit; it is getting "right inside the other person's skin." This kind of involvement hurts. Mercy isn't easy.

We noticed in another chapter that the Beatitudes sometimes seem to have a significant, logical order. It surely seems so in this instance. This Beatitude, "Happy are the merciful," follows immediately after "Happy are those who hunger and thirst after righteousness." Righteousness, admirable as it is, is always in danger of becoming hard; mercy is tender. Righteousness can easily turn inward, but mercy flows out. Righteousness can tend to become impatient with those who are not as hungry and as diligent in their quest; mercy is patience personified. After we have learned how to hunger and thirst for righteousness, we are ready to go on to mercy. Mercy, one might even say, is the higher righteousness.

I repeat, mercy costs us emotionally. You can't remain safely detached and objective when you feel mercy. Instead, you hurt with the other person. You feel their arthritis, their wart becomes your disfigurement, their fears become your terrors. But mercy is still more than an emotional reaction. Emotions can become a self-justifying cul-de-sac, going nowhere; true mercy requires action. It isn't enough to shed a tear of sympathy, though tears do help at times. But it's also possible to use tears to protect ourselves from investing in true Christian mercy. If we feel tenderhearted yet do nothing concrete to relieve the other person's need, our tenderheartedness can become inward and self-serving.

So with all that I've said about the emotional involvement that exists in true mercy, I have to go on to say that mercy is just as practical, as down-to-earth, and as dirty-your-hands-with-the-problem as it is emotional. It can be easy to think of mercy being dispensed at an impersonal, institutional level, but mercy is for all of us, and it calls for expression in the kitchen, office, and shopping mall. Some years ago I heard a theologian lecture on Christian concern for the poor and the underprivileged, then sat with him at a luncheon table where he was discourteous and difficult with his server. Apparently he saw mercy as a theological concept and didn't recognize its potential when it touched his coat sleeve.

Mercy is nothing if it isn't practical. I remember a story from another day when Jacob Bright came upon a poor neighbor on the road whose horse had been injured and now must be destroyed. People, in all good intentions and concern, were crowding about, expressing their sympathy. One man was especially verbose in showing his pity. Suddenly Jacob Bright said, "I am sorry five pounds' worth. How much are you sorry?" and he began taking up a collection to buy the man a new horse. When we express our sorrow over the plight of another, here is a good, very practical question: *How much am I sorry? How many dollars' worth, or how many hours, or in what deed?*

Most of us meet needs for mercy daily, and in many instances we hardly know that these needs exist. Some years ago Billy Graham accepted the invitation of a friend to join him in a Christmas Eve distribution of gifts in the nearby North Carolina mountains. Recalling the experience, Dr. Graham said:

> I thought everybody in our community had all the necessities of life. But I was taken back into some little mountain valleys where people did not have enough to wear, enough

to eat, and could not even afford soap to wash their bodies. Appalled and humbled, I asked God to forgive me for neglecting the people in my own community. I had not even bothered to look around me to see what people's needs were.

I doubt that any of us can begin to imagine the needs for mercy that exist in our own city or community. Some get close enough to the poverty of an area or its medical needs to evaluate the more obvious scene; but who knows what inward pain the person in the service station or the beauty parlor or the person sitting next to us at a faculty meeting or in our church pew may be enduring? In most instances they're not going to tell us about their problem; nevertheless, the pain of life would be relieved in some measure if more mercy were shown, the measure that demonstrates itself in normal kindness, in patience of listening, in warm friendliness. In busy days I have to remind myself of this fact, and I worry that sometimes I don't succeed in making myself fully attentive. Each of us, you see, has opportunities to extend mercy—human kindness—many times a day. And mercy is a kind of spiritual wonder drug, in that it bypasses all the other organs to go directly to the point of need. We don't need to know the specifics of someone's need in order to be a messenger of mercy. Indeed, we may not even know that a need exists. But as we relate to a person in merciful kindness, the mercy finds its way directly to the place of pain.

And here's something that may perhaps surprise you. True mercy is difficult not only because of its emotional and practical demands, but also because of its intellectual demands. Since mercy has so much to do with our affective natures, we're likely to overlook its intelligence elements. Because while good will seems often to express itself in simple ways, it is often very complex in the judgments it forces upon us. Take the story with which I began this chapter. The medical executive was urging the young doctor to exercise mercy; but suppose that older doctor continued to err—what would be the effect on future patients?

Sometimes we think we're being merciful when we're only being muddleheaded. Suppose I'm serving on a jury: if I am merciful to the defendant, will I do so at the expense of the injured party? If one of my students is doing poor work, am I merciful in letting him or her feel that the work is better than it is? Will that student ever have the opportunity to grow if my intended mercy hides his failings? When a child needs discipline, is it merciful to withhold the discipline—or might it be more merciful to enforce discipline?

Mercy, you see, must be intelligent if it really has the other person's welfare—and the welfare of the larger society—in mind. As the late G. L. Studdert-Kennedy said, mercy in a strange way is sometimes contrary to justice. Thus mercy is never easy, and rarely is it simple.

It's easy to agree with this fifth Beatitude. We want to obtain mercy because we need it, and we often like to extend it because it makes us feel noble, and rightly so. But we forget how difficult it may be to extend mercy to others. Because in order to be merciful, we have to pay a high emotional, practical, and intellectual price.

So mercy isn't easy. If it were (as I said earlier), we would practice it more often. Mercy is one of the most divine qualities that we humans are allowed—and commanded—to exercise. When we're merciful, we imitate our Lord, whose mercy is unfailing—"new every morning," as the Old Testament saint said (Lamentations 3:22-23). And the opportunities for the exercise of mercy are all around us; almost everywhere we look, someone wants mercy, longs for it, desperately needs it, even though the cry may be inaudible or the need unseen.

It should, in truth, be easy for you and me to respond. After all, we have received mercy. When we call ourselves

Christians we thus identify ourselves as recipients of God's ultimate mercy. Wealthy, then, in our store of mercy received, we go forth to share our wealth with others whose lives are currently poor. It's a privileged way to live. It's part of the beatific life.

12/0 3/08

My
Discussion

CHAPTER 8

Heartfelt Joy

12/10/08

"Blessed are the pure in heart, for they will see God."

Read Matthew 5:8.

Brian Doyle calls the human heart "the wet engine." It's a playful title, but also a very serious one. The heart is, in truth, an engine, perhaps the oldest one on our planet; a wonderful mechanism that goes night and day whether we're waking or sleeping, distributing thousands of gallons of blood through the body. It works ceaselessly and untiringly, with no vacations and no rest periods. But as wonderful as our human heart is, in a sense it is no more wonderful than the heart of a hummingbird, which beats ten times a second yet is no bigger than a pencil eraser. By inconceivable contrast, the heart of a blue whale—the largest heart on our planet—weighs more than seven tons.[1] But whether human, hummingbird, or blue whale, the heart is basically an engine, doing its absolutely essential but really rather monotonous work.

But after all this has been said about the heart as an engine, all of us will agree that this description isn't really enough. From time beyond memory, we humans have seen something else in the heart. I suspect it's because the heart seems to respond to emotional stimulation of almost every kind, which gives us the impression that the heart is somehow, in some way, almost mystical. In any event, most of us will nod in agreement when Doyle describes the heart as "the wet engine from which comes all the music we know."[2] So we understand why a wise person three or four thousand years ago said, "Keep your heart with all vigilance, / for from it flow the springs of life" (Proverbs 4:23). You and I think of the heart, symbolically at least, as the center of our emotions, our loyalties, and our crucial decisions. Indeed, the biblical writers went farther than that; they used the heart to describe the whole human personality, including will and character as well as emotions.

No wonder, then, that Jesus' description of the happy life includes a reference to the heart: "Happy [are] the pure in heart: / they shall see God" (Matthew 5:8 JB). We quickly agree, but even while this phrase, with its innate poetry, rolls so easily from our tongues, we have to acknowledge that it doesn't really have much credence in our contemporary culture. None of its elements make sense to persons shaped largely by the media. Other generations may often enough have ignored purity but they nevertheless considered it a virtue. Nowadays it's more often smiled on condescendingly and sometimes even scorned. As for purity bringing happiness, even some who endorse purity hardly believe that it's the way to happiness; they think rather that purity is a discipline to be endured. Nor does the reward promised by Jesus—the privilege of seeing God— hold much appeal to the general populace. I fear that a majority of our contemporaries have so dulled their God-consciousness that the seeing of God isn't really a major life goal. In eternity, yes, but not necessarily on this planet.

But even in the face of such judgments, I dare to say that few subjects in our time are as important as this one. Critics of the church often say that we should be more "relevant," whatever that code word may mean. Well, here is a relevant theme, you can be sure of that. Impurity of heart may be the paramount sickness of our time, so that in turn, purity of heart may be our greatest single need.

First of all, let's try to see what the Bible means by the term "purity of heart." The New Testament word for *pure* is the Greek word *katharos*. As you speak that word aloud you probably guess that it's the ancestor of our words *catharsis* and *cathartic*. As the Greeks used it in Jesus' day, the word meant simply *clean*, and it was used to describe soiled clothing that had been washed. The Greeks also used this word to describe grain that had been winnowed and sifted and thus rid of chaff. And here's an interesting usage: the Greeks applied this word to describe an army after it had been purged of all its discontented, cowardly, or ineffective soldiers.[3]

So you see, when the New Testament speaks of a pure heart, it is speaking of a heart that has been purged and cleansed so that it is unadulterated and unspoiled. The penetrating Danish philosopher, Søren Kierkegaard, said that purity of heart is "to will one thing." That is, purity means an utter singleness of life and purpose.

I suspect I should stop to underline the word *heart*. The purity we're talking about just now is purity of *heart*. That's more, you see, than sexual purity, important as that is; and more too than purity of words, thought, or deeds. Purity of heart is larger by far than any of these specific elements; it includes all of life. When we speak of purity of heart in its biblical sense, we mean thought and conduct, body and mind, sex and conversation, reading and viewing and hearing, deed and dream.

Such purity has always been hard to come by, but I dare to think that the problem is intensified in our day. Everything in our culture seems to be against purity. After all, we have to live in our culture, and at times it seems that we are nothing less than prisoners of the culture. We're surrounded by a certain style of life, and it seeks constantly, both openly and subtly, to press us into its mold. Because it is the culture of the times we are largely unconscious of its continuing influence. Some of us with a longer memory will pause at times to compare this time with other periods in which we have lived—and sometimes we're startled to see that matters which once seemed abhorrent to us have now become commonplace. So it is that a culture shapes us. And if that is so for those of us who have known other culture patterns, what basis of discrimination exists for those whose only cultural experience is the one they now know? We are fed an almost constant diet of easy violence, easy sex, easy classroom cheating, indifferent human relationships, and constant distractions. In such a setting, with such a daily menu of sight, sound, and experience, it is difficult (some would say impossible) to be pure in heart.

Consider, for one thing, how difficult it is to have singleness of mind in an environment that allows so little opportunity for contemplation. The average city dweller has few moments to examine his or her soul. The automobile, the radio and television, and piped-in music, the Internet, and now the cell phone that for many people is essentially an evolutionary appendage to the body—and worse, the soul!—add up all these, and ask yourself where the soul can have the privacy to examine itself. When is there opportunity to analyze our motives and to chart the soul's course, so that we can contemplate what is pure and what is not? The great saints of past ages contended that the godly life depended upon having much time for quiet contemplation. It looks as if we'll have to find a new formula in our contemporary world, because everything in our culture wars against such private places.

To complicate matters still further, the prevailing mood of our world is secular. The emphasis is heavily on the material, the sensual, and the here and now. Much of what occupies us is not patently bad; it's just that it crowds out the consideration of God. A person can quite easily go days without hearing the name of God except as that name is taken in vain. Sometimes faithful churchgoers complain that they hear little of God and the Bible even when they go to church. It is probably true that there have been generations when the churches seemed indifferent to the needs of the present world because they were so absorbed with the world to come. Now it often seems that our preaching is so occupied with the problems of this world that we neglect God and matters eternal.

When it comes to purity of heart as it expresses itself in traditional issues of morality, it is hard to believe or to evaluate properly what has happened in the past two decades. Words that were once found only in the washrooms of bus stations are now standard fare in many popular novels and in a great many channels of the television screen. Obscenity and pornography are hard put to find something shocking enough to get below the common levels of depravity.

And with all of this lifestyle what is perhaps worst is that many will suggest simply that purity is naïve. They won't argue that purity is a bad thing; it's just not cognizant of the "real world." Purity isn't taken seriously. Therefore it isn't likely to die from opposition in the field of battle but from neglect—neglect, even, by its friends. There have been periods in history when great numbers of persons made purity the main business of their lives. At such times there was more incentive for the larger population to seek the pure heart. In our time, by painful contrast, the heart that is singularly attentive to God is unheralded and almost unknown. A pessimist might conclude that such a heart might easily become extinct.

At this point a tough-minded rationalist might ask what difference that would make. In truth, not one of us, not even the worst of us, would want to live in a world where purity didn't exist. The pure in heart may not be very obvious in our world; they may seem as obscure as that lovely character in Robert Browning's poem "Pippa Passes." But unnoticed as such persons may be, the pure in heart are society's redeeming factor. The pure in heart are the redemptive leaven in our world, the leaven that keeps our culture from losing all semblance of flavor. They help the mediocre to be better, and they keep the corrupt from simply destroying society.

Because you see, no one wants to live in an utterly immoral, impure world. The person who lives by lying hopes that other people will tell the truth, otherwise his lies will get no hearing—just as the counterfeiter is out of business unless there is true currency in the world. The drunken driver hopes he or she is driving in a world of sober drivers, and the tax-dodger counts on it that most people are paying their way because if everyone were like him, the economy would collapse. The impure are leeches on society, depending on others to keep their world safe so they can practice their kind of irresponsibility. So the whole world depends, whether we acknowledge it or not, on the uplifting, redeeming influence of the pure in heart. Without such purity, the world would collapse of its own weight of crudeness and irresponsibility.

So what do the pure in heart get out of all this? What is their reward for paying their taxes while others cheat, for speaking the truth in the midst of lies, for seeking purity when the weight of influence around them is so often seductive and crude? They get a special kind of happiness—the vision of God. "How happy are the pure in heart: they shall see God."

I suspect this is the point at which you conclude that I'm talking about heaven, and ultimately I am. If there's anything in you that believes in a world to come, the idea of heaven carries a great deal of weight. And of course you see the logic of it: it's hard to imagine impurity in heaven.

But I want just now to talk about *this* world, because this is the one in which you and I have to live out our purity. And I want to insist that the pure in heart see God in this life, in the here and now, in ways that the general populace can't really imagine. The fact is, all of us see what we are conditioned to see, and we hear what we are conditioned to hear. The person who is hard of hearing does pretty well as long as others are talking about matters with which they are familiar, because that's what they're expecting to hear. Or to present it another way, someone with quite excellent hearing will ask to have an unfamiliar name repeated simply because the name, by its unfamiliarity, is difficult to hear. We hear best what is most familiar to us.

Ralph W. Sockman made this point by way of an incident from the life of the great English landscape artist, J. M. W. Turner. A sightseer, looking over Turner's shoulder while he was at work, said, "Why, Mr. Turner, I never saw any such light and color in nature as you put in your canvas." Turner replied, "Don't you wish you could? As for me, I never can hope to match with pigments the glory I see in the sky."[4] And of course that's the point. The artist sees colors in the sky that I don't see, and the musician hears notes in the symphony that never reach my ears. We perceive what we have carefully trained ourselves to perceive—and in those areas of our lives where we have no training (or perhaps more likely, no desire to learn) we may perceive next to nothing.

And so it is that the pure in heart *see God.* By the singleness of the longing that develops purity in the heart and mind, those with a pure heart train themselves to grasp realities that the average person misses completely. Walk down a noisy city street with a friend who loves nature and that friend is likely to lay a hand on your arm and ask, "Did you hear that?" He or she heard a bird, a cricket, a gentle voice of nature hidden to the hurrying pedestrians. Walk someday with the pure in heart, and even in the most raucous, godless culture, such a person will lay a hand on yours and say, "See: there is God! God is at work in our world." The pure in heart are sensitive to the reality of God to a degree that most of us are not. The pure in heart, as a result, *see God.*

In a sense, this Beatitude is, as the saying goes, a no-brainer. God is the ultimate expression of purity, so who would be able to see God except those who are pure? After all, we see through the lens of what we are; so only the pure are equipped for the beatific vision. Saint Augustine explained that "to see" carries the idea of *comprehending;* who else can comprehend God but those who are pure in heart? We need such purity if we are to see without moral distortion.

In his book *Pathways to Happiness,* the late Leonard Griffith asked, "Does it matter that we see God in all the circumstances of life?" then proceeded to answer his own question: "Does anything else matter? Until we see God, life has no rational meaning."[5] To go through life without seeing God is like someone never hearing music or harmony, only incessant noise—only far worse. To go through life without seeing God is to miss the point of it all, both here and in the world to come.

So how important is purity? In a measure, this depends on how deep the conscience is. That is, can we ever run away from ourselves? Can we escape something that is planted deep within us by the Creator, something so much a part of us that it will make its demands on us someday, somewhere, somehow? Could it be that much of the illness of us modern creatures—our enmity from person to person, our primal insecurity, and the division within our own souls—is in a profound sense a result of our impurity? Could it be that, not having a pure, single aim in life, we are split and harried, no matter what else we are or think or achieve? If so, then short of eternity itself, impurity of heart is the most serious form of our human problem.

In that case, here is the big question: *How do we get purity of heart?* George Buttrick said that this Beatitude is "the most inaccessible" of all the Beatitudes. But when I think of the persons I've known who seem to me to come closest to purity of heart, I have seen persons who have centered their affections on Jesus Christ. I have come to feel that there is great wisdom in the simple exhortation of the hymn that asks us to turn our eyes upon Jesus, because in doing so other claims will "grow strangely dim."[6]

Jesus Christ is the great fascination. Given half a chance, he captures us. And with him, we get the singleness and the wholeness in life that makes for purity of heart. Seeing him, we see God, and the wet engine plays the music of heaven.

CHAPTER *9*

A Very Happy Business 12/17/08

" Blessed are the peacemakers,
for they will be called sons of
God "

Read Matthew 5:9.

On Wednesday morning, December 2, 1942, a group of scientists completed an experiment in a converted squash court in Chicago. From a scientific point of view they had completed a monumental achievement. From a historical point of view, they had turned a corner in the story of humanity. Out of their discovery was to come the atomic bomb and the unleashing of a whole new arsenal of power. One person in that select group was the Nobel Prize-winning physicist Arthur Compton. As Dr. Compton recalled the occasion years later, he said that he felt a sense of gratitude to God for another of God's great gifts, but that he knew this was a gift that could put a question mark over humanity's future. Professor Compton then said, "Man must now go the way of Jesus or perish."[1]

In my childhood, a statement like Dr. Compton's was the sort of thing one heard primarily—perhaps exclusively!— from preachers. In this twenty-first century, physical scientists, sociologists, and political scientists have joined the company of the prophets. They remind us that there is no future in war, no future in hate, no future in revenge. Any attempt we make to destroy others will almost surely turn and destroy us. Do you remember the words of Tevye in the delightful musical *Fiddler on the Roof?* It was the year 1905 and a Russian government official had just advised the little Jewish community in a remote Russian village that they must get out of the land in three days or be destroyed. One of Tevye's Jewish friends cried out in anger against the injustice. "We should defend ourselves. An eye for an eye, a tooth for a tooth." To which Tevye, the dairyman, replies, "Very good. And that way, the whole world will be blind and toothless."[2] In our time of sophisticated weapons we have to update Tevye's words: if we insist on fighting one another, the whole world will soon be lifeless.

Nearly twenty centuries ago, in a time that on the surface seems simpler than our own, Jesus included peace as part of his grand formula for the happy life. Since we call Jesus the Prince of Peace, we aren't surprised that he said, "Blessed are the peacemakers, for they will be called children of God" (Matthew 5:9).

But as we have seen in the other Beatitudes we have discussed, we are easily inclined to read Jesus' words in a superficial way and thus miss the point altogether. It seems so natural to sift Jesus' teachings through our own prejudices and preconceptions until we hear him saying what we already have in mind. In this instance, for example, we're likely to think instinctively that Jesus said, "Happy are those who are at peace." Now mind you, it's very desirable to be at peace; I covet such a state of mind for both you and me. But Jesus is saying something far bigger, and in truth something quite unsettling. He is calling us to a difficult, heroic way of life: "Happy are the *peacemakers.*" We reason that happiness means enjoying peace; Jesus tells us that it lies in *making* peace.

So what did Jesus have in mind? To understand him, we should no doubt begin with the key word, *peace.* Jesus grew up with a great Hebrew word, *shalom.* For the Jew, this was a word of greeting and farewell; it was "hello" and "good-bye," "howdy" and "so long," "great to see you," and "see you later." I repeat, *shalom* was both greeting and farewell, with a one-word translation: *peace.* You greeted a friend by wishing him or her peace and you sent the person on the way with good wishes of peace.

That's lovely. But what did the word mean? What was there about this word that made generations of Jews use it for beginnings and endings, as a kind of blessed bookend to any meeting, whether casual or planned? When we speak of peace we instinctively have in mind the absence of war or strife; that is, we see peace not as a quality in itself but as freedom from a negative state. The Hebrew word, however, was a very positive word, meaning "everything which makes for a [person's] highest good."[3] One Jewish scholar said that the word means, in a sense, "completed, fulfilled." Thus when a person bid farewell to a friend by saying, "Shalom," he or she was in truth saying something like, "may you be filled out," or "may you be completed."

So the Hebrew word for peace—a word that was so much a part of Jesus' life, as greeting and farewell—was a very strong word. We're inclined, unfortunately, to see many religious words as weak, passive, or even rather negative. Thus we picture humility as an absence of pride rather than a word strong in its own right, and virtue as an absence of sin, when in truth there's so much more to virtue than the avoidance of evil. We rarely realize that goodness is a powerful, affirmative force, the strongest force in the world. Goodness has survived over the millennia even though evil seems so powerful. Even so, peace in a biblical sense is not simply the silencing of guns, it is a state of well-being, of fullness. The late George Buttrick said that what we call peace is usually not peace at all, "but only smoldering grudges and exhausted hatreds."[4] And therein lies a large part of our human problem: we bring an end to armed conflict but we leave a vacuum where perhaps even greater conflicts can take root and grow. True peace is not a vacuum, but a fullness.

And of course Jesus was talking about far more than international relations. I don't by any means want to minimize the constant peril of war between nations. Other than poverty, war is no doubt the greatest single physical source of human suffering. I mean only to remind us that issues of peace are concerned with far more than military conflict; peace is at issue in every kind of circumstance and human relationship. If by a miracle of diplomacy we could bring international conflict to an end, we would still need peacemakers to deal with all the other troubled places in our lives. I think of the old story about the soldier who wrote from a battlefield to some family member, "Please stop nagging me, so I can fight this war in peace!" As a matter of fact, some off-battlefield conflicts are more complicated in their own way than the stuff of international negotiation.

If we're to be true to what Jesus taught, and if we are to find the kind of peace that really matters—the kind encompassed by the Beatitude—we will have to work with a broad and very positive definition of peace. We would do well to begin by finding peace in our individual, inner lives—not because this was the point of the Beatitude but because we're not in a very good position to make peace beyond ourselves when we don't have peace within ourselves. Then we can progress to those other levels of peacemaking: husband and wife, parent and child, roommate and roommate, employer and employee, neighbor and friend, rich and poor, server and diner, clerk and customer, interracial and intraracial.

As I read the admittedly incomplete list that I've just recorded, I realize how much of our energy we spend in making not peace, but war. Let's look at it this way. Nearly all the activity in the world's courtrooms is invested in the conflicts with which we live, whether person and person or corporation and corporation. So, too, with so much of the business we bring to counselors and to consultants. A great many persons are nothing less than walking battle-fields, so occupied by psychic, internal strife that it's no wonder they start little daily wars in the world in which they live. Nor is it too surprising that some of the persons who crusade for a world free from war are impossible to live with on a one-to-one basis. We humans seem to have a commitment to conflict.

And to all of us very human persons, Jesus said, "Happy are the peacemakers!" Making peace is a very happy busi-ness. After all, what occupation could be more satisfying than to invade situations of destruction and turn them into settings of beauty and fulfillment? Peacemakers, Jesus said, shall be called "children of God." That is, they shall be called *godly*, partakers of the very nature of God. That's really quite logical, because one must be very godlike to step into chaos and establish order.

But how exactly does one *make* peace? Nearly all of us claim to want peace; even those who declare war often do so with the claim that their intent is to establish a basis for a lasting peace. Since peace is so universally admired and presumably so universally sought after, it must not be that easy to achieve, else our human race would have won the goal several millennia ago.

Let me start with the counsel of a great philosopher and theologian, the late William Temple, the notable Arch-bishop of Canterbury—the titular head of the Anglican Church by office, but one of the most significant voices of Christianity in the twentieth century simply by the strength of his scholarship and integrity. During World War II in a broadcast to the English people, Temple said, "This world can be saved from political chaos and collapse by one thing only, and that is worship."[5] I realize even as I write these words that some readers are shaking their heads at my political and military naiveté. And when I think of the rancor one sometimes finds in religious conventions or in local churches, I admit readily that the evidence makes my point seem painfully unrealistic. I know well enough that we humans can easily misuse prayer and worship. Nevertheless, I ponder the great souls over the centuries who have demonstrated by their lives that worship is the surest way to get ourselves into true alignment with our universe.

And it is at this point that we are ready for a second step toward peacemaking: finding peace with God and with ourselves. Most of us realize that we have conflicts within our own person—angers, resentments, bitterness, and fears. These inner conflicts easily break out upon the people or the groups with whom we associate. Henry C. Link, the psychologist to whom I referred in earlier chapters, told of a young woman and her mother who were in constant conflict with the rest of their family, even to the point of breaking up the family unit. Ironically, however, the young woman was "an ardent advocate of world peace," and her principal social activity was a society for the prevention of war.

Dr. Link said that he was tempted to ask the woman how she could expect to stop war between nations when she couldn't stop them in her own family. He then continued, "The psychologist finds the seeds of war, poverty, and discontent deep-seated in the inferiority, selfishness, and emotional instability of the individual." This conflict, Dr. Link continued, may be with another member of the family or within one's own person. Then he added:

> One of the most common symptoms of an inferiority complex or of personal failure is the desire to change the social order, usually in one's immediate environment, often in the world at large. The youngsters, suffering from personal failure, often want to change their families, not themselves. The student who fails in his studies wants to change his teachers or the marking system, not himself. The employee who fails to get the desired salary wants to improve his employer, not himself.[6]

Of course we can't postpone service to others or concern for world and social problems until we ourselves have reached personal perfection. But we would do well to search our own souls while we seek to correct others; it's a demonstration of Jesus' rule that we need to remove the beam from our own eye before we can take the moat from the eye of another. And we need to face the disarming possibility that perhaps we are working to reform others as a shield against dealing with our own shortcomings.

But if I seem to oppose organized social reform, let me hasten to say that peacemakers are desperately needed at such levels of persuasion and influence. This leads to my third recommendation, that if we are to be peacemakers in community or world affairs, we will almost surely have to affiliate with some larger movement. An organized body can accomplish goals that none of us can do alone. There is strength in community.

Since my life has been spent in the life of the church, I am prejudiced by experience for working with the community of faith. I suspect that we often overlook the church's peacemaking efforts, partly because we have too small a definition of peacemaking and often because we take the work of the church for granted. As a pastor, I was privileged several times to help settle refugee families in America, where they could recover from the war and dislocation they had suffered. I think of what is often referred to as the Heifer Program, an admirable project for combating world hunger—started by one of the great peace churches. And then there's Habitat for Humanity, a program that began with one man's powerful conversion and his increasing vision for empowering the poor. To be in the church is—at least potentially—to be in the peacemaking business. And it is a lovely business, indeed.

Then, especially, I urge that you and I would realize our potential for making peace through simple acts of kindness. So many folks could become instruments of peace in our world if only their own hearts weren't so possessed by resentment and self-centeredness. Kindness from others might begin to break the chains of hate that imprison such individuals. Francis of Assisi's great prayer, "Make me an instrument of thy peace," is nothing other than a quest for healing kindness in all the ordinary patterns of daily life. Saint Francis saw that there was hatred in the world, so he prayed that he might show love where hatred currently reigned. Because he saw sadness in the world, he asked that he might bring joy in its place. This remarkable man, this holy dreamer, realized that being an instrument of God's peace is a wide-ranging assignment, covering all of life. If we try to follow Saint Francis's counsel in our time and place, we will discover that there are opportunities every day to enlarge the borders of peace. If we see ourselves as peacemakers, we will dedicate the common stuff of our daily living—from a smile at a clerk to a friendly gesture in traffic to a letter to a senator—to the healing of our human race.

You see, each one of us has literally dozens and dozens of opportunities every day, every single day, to make peace in our world. What we need, most of all, is to be sensitive enough to see our opportunities, and to be close enough to God that we will then choose to use our energy, our personality, our money, and our influence to make a difference. That is, to be makers of peace.

And here is a big secret. If we are to be sensitive to the business of peacemaking, we will need to be persons of prayer. When we pray we wage peace at the most strategic level, because in prayer we deal with the hurt of the world at its essential core. But understand this: when we pray for peace, we have to pray without human prejudice. We cease to take sides. We pray for God's will to be done, and we pray for the welfare of our enemies as well as our own. I'm not suggesting that both sides in any conflict are equally right, although I would remind us that in most human conflicts it is exceedingly rare for one side to be one hundred percent right because we humans are all imperfect creatures. So we pray with humility, with readiness to repent, and with concern for those who have wronged us, even as we seek to understand if perhaps we have wronged the other party.

There's a very happy business right where you and I live that is just waiting to be done: making peace. Mind you, it isn't simple; that's why even the greatest of world leaders, including our religious, political, and intellectual leaders, fumble at the business.

It goes beyond political systems, beyond national boundaries, and beyond issues of wealth, culture, and intellect. It's a business that is open to every human being. Those who practice it daily—indeed, hourly—are among the happiest people on our planet. Because, after all, when we are peacemakers we are the *children of God,* part of the very family of heaven. I can't imagine a happier place to be.

CHAPTER 10

1/07/09

Merry Martyrs

Read Matthew 5:10-12.

*A*s we work our way through these remarkable sen-
tences that we call the Beatitudes, I suspect that
we're all beginning to realize that each Beatitude
compels us to rethink our definitions—definitions of life in
general and of happiness in particular. As I warned us earlier in our study, it's hardly necessary to find a back side
approach to the Beatitudes because they're already so contrary to our way of looking at life.

But among all the back-side aspects of the Beatitudes,
none is more pronounced than this last of the Beatitudes,
the crown and climax of the series. We get the point best in
the down-to-earth clarity of the phrasing in *The Living Bible*:

> "Happy are those who are persecuted because they are
> good, for the Kingdom of Heaven is theirs.
> "When you are reviled and persecuted and lied about
> because you are my followers—wonderful! Be *happy* about
> it! Be *very glad!* for a *tremendous reward* awaits you up in
> heaven. And remember, the ancient prophets were perse-
> cuted too." (Matthew 5:10-12 TLB)

Be happy because you're persecuted. That's a bit much. Finding happiness in persecution seems at best impossible and at worst a kind of masochism, the sort of attitude that calls for personality adjustment.

Before I go farther I must offer a personal caveat. I have no firsthand experience with persecution. I have preached several times in places where Christian witness was severely restricted by the government, but I have never lived day in, day out where my bodily freedom and safety were in danger because of possible arrest, abuse, or death. The first-century Christians knew what Jesus meant, and so do literally millions of twenty-first century believers in a number of places in the world. But my experience is minimal. In my junior high, high school, and college years I was sometimes an outsider because of my standards of personal conduct, and over the years I've received some pretty nasty anonymous mail from people who didn't like my convictions about personal, social, economic, or political morality. And some folks have made it clear that they think the world would be better off if I were removed from the planet, but no one has seriously threatened to see to my elimination, so I confess that I don't really know a lot about high-grade persecution.

But that doesn't give me the right to skip this Beatitude. You'll note that I've titled this chapter "Merry Martyrs." I'm not trying to be cute or mildly sensational, and I don't mean to use exaggerated language. Rather, I'm trying to convey accurately what the Beatitude says in the original text. The New Testament word that is usually translated "exceeding glad" comes from two Greek words which mean literally "to leap exceedingly."[1] To put it simply but clearly, we're talking about the kind of joy that sets a person to dancing. When you're persecuted—Wheeee! It's a reason to leap about. That's the mood of this word.

However, we'll never understand the reason for such radical happiness unless we put our own emphasis on the key phrases in this Beatitude: Happy are those who are persecuted *because they are good*—and again, "Blessed are you when people revile you and persecute you and utter all kinds of evil against you *falsely on my account*" (Matthew 5:11, emphasis added). The promise of this ecstatic joy isn't simply because one is being persecuted; it's about being persecuted for the right reason—persecution that comes because we are truly *good*; attacks that spring from false reasons but basically because of our commitment to Jesus Christ.

There's always the danger, you see, that we are fooling ourselves or that we will try to do so. Listen to Dr. Ralph Sockman: "The first value of persecution is to induce self-examination in order to find out why others dislike us."[2] It's quite possible, you know, that people are treating us badly not because of our goodness but because of lapses in our goodness—perhaps, for instance, that fatal lapse in righteousness that is termed *un*righteousness. A difficult and contentious person once complained to her pastor, "Nobody in my office likes me, because I'm such an outspoken Christian." In a reckless moment of candor her pastor replied, "Not really. I suspect it's because you're so unpleasant." I recall a time, early in my Christian life, when I became unduly impressed with my piety. My schoolmates were surprisingly kind to me. As I look back on those days I think some of my classmates who professed little or no religion may have demonstrated more Christian grace than I, with my religious experience, did.

Nevertheless, as Saint Paul wrote to his young disciple, Timothy, "Indeed, all who want to live a godly life in Christ Jesus will be persecuted" (2 Timothy 3:12). Sometimes persecution has come in the form of brutal physical torture. Emperor Nero in the first century A.D. seemed to stretch his imagination to find new ways to make Christians suffer. He covered them with pitch, then set them afire and used them as living torches to light his gardens. He sewed some in skins of animals, then set his hunting dogs upon them to tear them apart. Their eyes were torn out, or parts of their bodies amputated; others were tortured on the racks.

And Nero was not the last to indulge in such madness. Martyrdom was almost commonplace at repeated intervals during several early generations of the Christian church. In the third century Tertullian wrote, "The more ye mow us down, the more we grow. The blood of the martyrs is the seed of the Church." Men and woman have died for the Christian faith in every century since Stephen was stoned by a first-century mob. Now we're told that our own twentieth and twenty-first centuries are seeing more martyrs than any previous centuries of human history. Twice each year I am privileged to teach a select group of Christian leaders from other parts of the world. In some instances, these people go back to ministries where their lives are in peril every day. Their converts enter the same arena of hazard. Each time I leave these students I remind myself that while I have tried to teach them how to preach, they have taught me how to be a Christian.

But most of us who read this book are living in a culture where there's no danger of physical persecution. This could change, though at present it seems unlikely. Other persecution, however, does exist. Reputable businesses want honorable employees, but I've known men who lost their jobs because they could not in Christian conscience do what their employers required. Some women have lost promotions because they wouldn't compromise their sexual integrity. Some people are dropped from the social scene because of their Christian convictions. I'm quite sure there are organizations whose members would hesitate to elect a convinced Christian to their presidency for fear he or she might complicate the style of operation within the organization.

And there is a good deal of evidence that students in many colleges and universities are likely to see some of their dearest convictions used as a source of amusement by lecturers, and that theology—which was once the queen of the sciences—is now seen as an intellectual imposter, and its advocates as second-rate scholars. This is not, by any means, like being burned at the stake, but it is the kind of persecution that challenges one's sense of self-worth and that may in the long run be deeply destructive.

In truth, a vast percentage of our contemporaries think that religion is fine as long as we keep it in its place—which, coldly speaking, means Sunday morning, Christmas, and Easter. As for Christmas, some hope we will merge that once unique day into a generic term like "the holiday season." So if you indicate that your Christian faith is the dominant factor in your life (and you see, if you take Jesus seriously, that's the definition of a Christian: someone for whom Jesus Christ is the dominant factor in life)—well, then, you're likely even in our broadly permissive culture to suffer the pain of subtle and sometimes not-so-subtle persecution. Even today your faith may cost you money, social contacts, a job, promotions. In time, this may well get worse.

Of course, it's easy to avoid persecution. Two generations ago a young man took a summer job in a logging camp. His mother feared that the rough, rugged crowd with whom her son would be working might abuse the boy for his Christian convictions.

When he returned home at summer's end, his mother asked, "Did the men pick on you for being a Christian?" The boy's face brightened. "Never. They never found out."

The preacher in me must add, and neither did that young man find the happiness in being persecuted, even in the good-natured way of rough workers. He never experienced the unique gladness of a merry martyr.

"How *happy* are those who are persecuted for righteousness' sake," Jesus said, and history offers its proofs. One thinks of Edmund Campion, for whom the Campion Medal for distinguished literature is named. He was banished to the Tower of London for his faith, and three times was tortured on the rack in order to compel him to deny his witness. Then he was sentenced to be hanged, drawn, and quartered. When he received the sentence, he broke into the *Te Deum*—"We praise thee, O God." On a heavy, rainy December morning he was dragged through the litter-ridden streets of London to the place of execution (ironically, by persons who also identified themselves as Christians). The late William Sangster wrote of him, "He went up the cart at the place of execution as though he were going to a wedding."[3]

Some people are martyrs at secondhand, so to speak. Many years ago I knew a businessman who gladly gave his son to crucial missionary service. Not many years later that remarkable young man was martyred by the very people he was trying to serve; I consider his parents to have been martyrs, too. Many of us hail the magnificent witness of the German pastor, Dr. Martin Niemoeller, in World War II. He was thrown into a concentration camp because of that witness. His father told an acquaintance:

> When you go back to America, do not let anyone pity the father and mother of Martin Niemoeller. Only pity any follower of Christ who does not know the joy that is set before those who endure the cross despising the shame. Yes, it is a terrible thing to have a son in a concentration camp. Paula here and I know that. But there would be something more terrible for us: if God had needed a faithful martyr, and our Martin had been unwilling.[4]

What can you say to faith like that? Only that the Beatitude is true: "Happy are those who suffer for righteousness' sake."

If you've read a little church history or if you're keeping up on international news of what is happening to Christians today, you know that our story is punctuated by statements of such extraordinary joy. Merry martyrs! And for every declaration at the time of death or the threat of death, there are hundreds, perhaps thousands, that are unrecorded, spoken by "average" believers in the midst of commonplace persecutions. Those commonplace experiences should not be minimized, however. It is their very commonness that deserves praise. The ultimate experiences call forth the best in people; there is in them a sense of nobility and of eternity. The everyday slights and mistreatments have no such glamour, only irritation. But the rule of the Beatitude still applies: "How happy are those who are persecuted for my sake."

But why? What is the blessing in suffering for the name of our Lord? What makes this suffering different than other suffering?

To begin with, the company you keep. Jesus said, "In the same way they persecuted the prophets who were before you." When you're persecuted for *goodness*, you become part of the aristocracy of both human and divine history. The eleventh chapter of the New Testament book of Hebrews gives the stories of notable persons of faith, then adds that there are others who should be mentioned, persons "of whom the world was not worthy." Our world is full of such great souls.

Come to think of it, if it were not for such great souls, our world wouldn't be worth much of anything. All that matters in our world is sustained for us by those who are *good*—so very good that their goodness is sometimes an offense to us, until we persecute them because of their very goodness. They are a magnificent company, and if you and I merit a place with them, we have reason to rejoice. Remember when you ran home in ecstasy because you had been chosen for a team, or a play or concert, or had been elected into a club? The next time you are persecuted for being good, shout the wonderful news to your spouse or your closest friend: "Look what's happened to me! I've been elected into the company of heaven's noble ones!"

But that's only an incidental reason for happiness as this Beatitude sees it. The wondrous reason that Jesus gives is this: "a tremendous reward awaits you in heaven."

This is the only Beatitude that promises a reward in heaven. Another Beatitude promises that we will possess the kingdom of heaven, and still another that we will see God, but we can reasonably interpret those rewards as happening in this world as well as in the next. This Beatitude, however, guarantees a reward in heaven.

Perhaps this helps set us straight. We too often think we should get all our rewards on earth. "I've tried my best," we say, "and what good has it done me? Other people who don't give a nod to God seem to come out better than I do." This may very well be so, and perhaps we shouldn't be surprised. Some of the settling of accounts will be in the world to come. Jesus said that there will be rewards in *heaven*.

Here is the ultimate declaration of justice. Not all accounts are settled on this earth. We should hardly expect them to be; you and I are eternal creatures, so it's logical that some of our business will be settled in heaven. All of us have seen that some wonderfully good people don't seem to get a proper return on their life's investments on this planet, but this isn't the end of our story. Christians are a people with the long view, what might be called the faith perspective. We do what we believe is right, not because we will get an increase in salary or because we will win the next ball game, but because we believe it is right. We're willing to wait for the reward, even if it means waiting until the world to come. This is because we believe in God, in justice and goodness, and in the world to come. We believe that God will reward goodness, and we're so confident of this that we don't mind waiting for it. And we're confident, too, that God is generous. So generous, in fact, that we can be leaping-happy in anticipation.

I don't know how many of those who read this book will ever suffer physical persecution for their faith. I certainly wouldn't encourage you to court pain, but in a world as volatile as ours one can't predict what the future might hold. But of this I am sure: physical persecution or not, all of us who follow Christ can expect some kind of persecution—perhaps in particular the sort of thing Jesus had in mind when he spoke of being "reviled and lied about." Because when we are truly good, people respond in one of two ways: either by admiring the goodness and seeking it for themselves, or by resenting it and hoping they can find something in us that they can malign and thus discredit the goodness. Their response is none of our concern. Our business is simply to follow our Lord, and to leave the results to him.

How happy are those who are persecuted for their *goodness*, who are accused falsely, for Jesus' sake! They belong to the noblest company of human history, in the line of the prophets of old and the saints of more recent centuries. They will be rewarded in heaven. Whatever they get or don't get in this world, they have a sure inheritance in heaven.

If we are never persecuted for our goodness, we should probably ask ourselves why not; and if we seem sometimes to be persecuted, we should be sure that it is because of goodness and not because of some less noble factor. And all the way, my wish for you and for me is happiness, true happiness! The kind of happiness that makes folks leap for joy.

CHAPTER 11

So Where Do We Begin?

I have said several times along the way that it is difficult
to look at the Beatitudes from the "back side"
because that's what the Beatitudes are all about: a
view of life that is so contrary to the way we understand it
that they seem to come to us from "the back side"—at
least, that is, when we compare the Beatitudes with the way
most of us understand life! The Beatitudes' approach
seems so utterly contrary to the impressions we get by way
of our newspapers, periodicals, television, Internet, and
casual conversation. I expect that some would make it even
stronger and would say that the Beatitudes are contrary
even to common sense.

Are we to take Jesus seriously when he urges us to be
meek, because the meek will inherit the earth? Did he
really expect us to welcome persecution? And how could
we expect ever to have such purity in heart that we could
see God? Then, from all of these ruminations comes a bigger and more pertinent question: *Was Jesus recommending a
way of life for his followers in our ordinary times, or was he simply
trying to whet our appetite for a world yet to come?* On the other
hand, if Jesus meant his counsel for this world, was he perhaps laying out a pattern for a select few, a company of
extraordinary people who, most of us gladly confess, are

better than we can ever hope to be? As a matter of fact, even as I write those words I realize that whatever Jesus had in mind, apparently not many of us have chosen to follow his counsel.

Of course we can point to some great souls in Roman Catholicism, like Francis of Assisi or Mother Teresa. Or in my Protestant, Methodist tradition, I think of Harry Denman. And most of us will add a person or two from our own experience. I remember from my boyhood the deaconesses at the Helping Hand Mission who were paid an utterly minimum salary and lived in what would best be described as an old-fashioned college dormitory—the kind of dormitory some of us remember before rooms were made larger with comforts added. And come to think of it, as I recall those deaconesses and others like them, they were a very happy lot. As I remember them, they made a good case for the Beatitude life.

But let me interrupt myself for a moment to discuss that key word: *happy*. These days some thoughtful people are advising us that happiness is much overrated. Maybe *happy* isn't the best word for our discussion. The New Testament generally concentrates on the concept of *joy*, something that has little or no connection with the *happenings* or *happenstances* of life. To take a phrase from a thoughtful secular study, "Happiness displaces pain, but joy embraces it."[1] That is, joy takes conquest of all the stuff of life, both good and bad, while happiness generally depends largely on circumstances.

It is very clear that the happiness of which Jesus speaks in the Beatitudes has little or nothing to do with outward circumstances. Indeed, beatific happiness flies in the face of circumstances—it insists on embracing our circumstances, and thus transforming them. The average person says that life is just one fool thing after another, while the Beatitude person—whether so expressing it or not—sees life as just one conquest after another.

I have known some economically poor people who have lived their lives this way—people who have learned to find joy in their state of life rather than in their occasions of escaping it. In this, ironically, they differ dramatically from persons who have a good deal more of this earth's benefits but who seem nevertheless to devote so much of their time escaping their lives rather than embracing them. I'm referring to the fact that so many seem to live for vacations, or special events, or opportunities to buy still another toy. Some of the economically poor seem better able to find their happiness in the *allness* of life, if I may coin a word. They live for where they are rather than living for escapes from where they are. This says something to the point Jesus was making, because Jesus was insisting that the very elements that we generally see as sources of distress are in truth the setting for happiness. But it takes a certain life attitude to make it so.

Consider, too, the drive for self-esteem that seems to control so many of us and that is a significant factor even for some of us who like to think we have our egos fairly well in check. Many parents feel that they can do nothing better for their children than to develop in them a "healthy" self-esteem. But in truth, most such efforts are not really developing self-esteem; they're developing esteem that depends on praise and the recognition of others, on social acceptance, and on certain attainments or possessions. But what can we say for self-esteem that depends upon the home or neighborhood in which we live, the automobile we drive, the position we hold in work or community, or the opinions of other people? Self-esteem of this kind depends on things outside the self that are expected to give worth to the self.

It's quite frustrating to the person whose pride rests in a certain automobile or boat when they come upon someone who hardly knows the difference between a small Volkswagen and a Rolls Royce. What good does it do to tell such a person about your car if he or she doesn't know that your automobile has special prestige? And how can you impress a person with your cultural references or your name-dropping if the other person doesn't envy you any of these matters? My point, quite simply, is this: true self-esteem, at its best, had better rest on something more than what we put on, drive, drink, wear, or flaunt; because if we're depending on these to make us happy with ourselves, our self isn't very secure. Mind you, I'm not disparaging true achievement or an honorable love of excellence and beauty; I'm only saying that if our sense of self-worth rests in these matters, our self is not very rich.

I think of Molly Bruce Jacobs's remarkable story of the sister she never really knew until she was thirty-eight years old and her sister was thirty-five. When Molly was thirteen her parents told her that this younger sister existed; but that in a pattern that was common at the time the parents had arranged for the girl, who has severe mental retardation, to be in a care facility with others whose lives were similarly limited.

But as Molly came to adult life and with it success in her demanding profession, she sought out her sister and began to visit her often. As she did so, she observed:

> In spite of her disabilities, she was everything I wasn't, or what I'd imagined I wasn't allowed to be. She exuded the joie de vivre that dries up in you when you're raised to believe that the trophies and rewards you accumulate will make you happy, and that the pursuit of truth and beauty is for only dreamers and fools.[2]

Reading Molly's rather poignant insight, I pondered in new light Jesus' counsel that we must "change and become like children" if we are to enter the kingdom of heaven (Matthew 18:3). Certainly the Beatitudes compel us to look at life in a quite naïve, trusting, childlike way. We abandon our sophistication, our "you've got to take care of number one" attitude, our acquisitiveness, and our fascination with the superficial if we take seriously the Beatitudes and the rest of the Sermon on the Mount. If we do so, many will judge us dreamers and fools—even while, in the deep of their souls, they may well wonder at us and envy us.

Somewhere in my reading or perhaps in some random discussion I have heard the Bible referred to as "reality according to God." That phrase is at once exotic and unbending, but it deserves our attention—especially as we look at the Beatitudes. You see of course that our problem with the Beatitudes is that they seem to us so out of touch with reality. J. Clinton McCann Jr. and James C. Howell say that any Sunday school teacher has found that when the Beatitudes are mentioned someone will say, "That's not the real world." Daily evidence probably seems to support that statement. But is it perhaps the world as it *ought* to be? And if it isn't the way everyone is going to live, or even the way a majority will live, is it nevertheless the way some of us should be living? And if we did so live, might God's reality then have at least a measure of exposure (and thus of credibility) in our world?

That is, should some of us become so deeply convinced that the Beatitudes are God's pattern of reality that we will try to live the Beatitudes, no matter what the majority do or think? Is it our responsibility as Christians to demonstrate a life that is out of the ordinary in its beauty, its strength, and its eternal practicality? Because, you see, Jesus was trying to convince us that the Beatitude way of life is not impractical; to the contrary, it is the only really practical way to live. Will we be able to persuade the whole world to live as Jesus taught? I don't know. I won't even venture to say that the Bible promises such an achievement outside of the time when there will be "new heavens and a new earth." But we do know that God expects us—those of us who take Jesus seriously—to make as much of a difference as is within our reach. And in truth, most of us underestimate our potential as influencers. There is more power in our daily witness of goodness than we can ever imagine.

I suspect that the greatest danger Christianity must cope

with is not, on the one hand, the opposition of tyrants who try to shut down churches and forbid missionaries, or on the other hand, the arguments of a certain type of intellectual who despises the church. These are of course forces to be reckoned with, and fearful ones. But they are more easily coped with because we can so easily identify them. Our greater hazard is in the way most of us, as Christians, have domesticated Christ and his teachings so that a thoughtful observer might confuse Christianity as we live it with almost any pleasant, well-meaning, rather bland, and superficial philosophy of life.

J. B. Phillips, the great Anglican priest of the mid-twentieth century and the person who blessed all of the English-speaking world with his modern language translation of the New Testament, saw it another way. He pleaded with the church "to get back to essential Christianity so that we may realize afresh the revolutionary character of its message." He then spoke a word that may well offend some of us. He said that we may have "allowed what we call 'Western civilization,' or 'the American way of life' to become more or less God-fearing substitutes for the real thing."

Phillips continues by bringing up the word I've mentioned several times in recent paragraphs, *reality*. "The reality, according to Jesus, is the establishment and growth of a Kingdom of inner loyalty which transcends all human barriers." And because this is reality, Phillips says that this is "the real significance of man's temporary existence upon the earth."[3]

That's a challenging word from a man who was in pursuit of sainthood. Let me bring in a secular voice that is quite as challenging, although couched with biting irony. Novelist Kurt Vonnegut, commenting on recurring appeals to post the Ten Commandments in public places, noted that no one seems to suggest doing so with the Beatitudes. " 'Blessed are the merciful' in a courtroom? 'Blessed are the peacemakers' in the Pentagon? Give me a break!"[4] A tough-minded, quite fearless Anglican priest from the first half of the twentieth century, G. A. Studdert-Kennedy, was as emphatic as Vonnegut, though in a different tone: "The standards of Christ are not arbitrary ideals for exceptional men, they are the bedrock necessities of social life, [that] we disobey at our peril."[5]

I see the Beatitudes as a divine attitude adjustment. They stop us short in our headlong chase for happiness, to ask if we aren't missing something. Is it just possible that our common sense keeps us from finding some wonderfully uncommon sense? Do we perhaps miss God because we insist on fencing God within the boundaries of a way of life that is more "average," more acceptable to a culture that prizes possessions and prestige and power?

I'm a religious professional, with nearly forty years as a pastor, then several years as a guest preacher and teacher, and more recently nearly a decade and a half as a seminary professor and administrator. I have tried through these professional years to remain an amateur; that is, to follow Christ as simply as I did when I started the journey as a ten-year-old. But it's a hard thing to bring off. And it's difficult not only for someone like me, who has been "paid to be good," it's also difficult for those who have been part of the Christian community long enough that they allow it to lose its challenging, demanding, radical voice.

The religious professionals in Jesus' day were upset when his followers threw robes and palm branches in his path when he entered Jerusalem. Jesus replied that if "these were silent, the stones would shout out" (Luke 19:40). Now and then, it seems to me, a stone does shout out, and we are bewildered by the sound. Stephen H. Webb, the fine contemporary theologian, has urged a rethinking of Jack Kerouac's novel *On the Road*. He admits that stylistically it was a flawed novel and that a great many young men found in it an excuse for excess and immaturity.

But Professor Webb reminds us that the term associated

with Kerouac and his novel, "beat"—as in "beat generation"—had a quite different meaning for Kerouac than is
generally thought. Kerouac coined the term after he had
received what he felt was a *beatific* vision in a Catholic
church in 1954. So where many of his readers saw his novel
as license for rebellious living, Kerouac was underscoring
the tragedy of immorality. "Sin is sin, and there's no erasing
it," he wrote. He shocked many of his admirers when he
confessed in an interview in *Paris Review* that all he ever
really wanted to write about was Jesus.[6]

Was Kerouac a "stone shouting"? I'm inclined to think so.
And even as I acknowledge that in some ways his shouting
may have done more harm than good, I get the uneasy feeling that his shouting came because we followers of Jesus
were silent. We have taken the edgy Jesus of the Beatitudes
and the Sermon on the Mount and have made him comfortable in our suburb.

At this point I know that some of you are happy you can
close this book, and that others are asking, "What, exactly,
do you want us to do?" If you want such a formula, I will dis-
appoint you. Something about the Beatitudes is too intimate
to allow me or any other teacher or preacher to apply its
specifics to anyone else. And this is partly because I find that
the Beatitudes and the Sermon on the Mount require me to
use all my moral energy for living them out in my own life.

But of this I am sure. Jesus was serious when he set out
these strange words from the back side, and he expected
his followers to take them seriously. I think he was content
in the realization that only a minority would do so. But he
knew that if that minority would become dedicated
enough, they would serve as leaven that would influence
the whole lump.

This is the conviction that impels me to press on; to seek
daily for the beatific vision that will help me live these back-
side Beatitudes so I can see the front side of the kingdom
of heaven.

The Beatitudes from the Back Side

JOHN D. SCHROEDER

This book by J. Ellsworth Kalas examines the Beatitudes, the series of blessings spoken by Jesus in the Sermon on the Mount. To assist you in facilitating a discussion group, this study guide was created to help make this experience beneficial for both you and members of your group. Here are some thoughts on how you can help your group:

1. Distribute the book to participants before your first meeting and request that they come having read the first chapter. You may want to limit the size of your group to increase participation.
2. Begin your sessions on time. Your participants will appreciate your promptness. You may wish to begin your first session with introductions and a brief get-acquainted time. Start each session by reading aloud the snapshot summary of the chapter for the day.
3. Select discussion questions and activities in

advance. Note that the first question is a general question designed to get discussion going. The last question is designed to summarize the discussion. Feel free to change the order of the listed questions and to create your own questions. Allow a set amount of time for the questions and activities.

4. Remind your participants that all questions are valid as part of the learning process. Encourage their participation in discussion by saying that there are no wrong" answers and that all input will be appreciated. Invite participants to share their thoughts, personal stories, and ideas as their comfort level allows.

5. Some questions may be more difficult to answer than others. If you ask a question and no one responds, begin the discussion by venturing an answer yourself. Then ask for comments and other answers. Remember that some questions may have multiple answers.

6. Ask the question "Why?" or "Why do you believe that?" to help continue a discussion and give it greater depth.

7. Give everyone a chance to talk. Keep the conversation moving. Occasionally you may want to direct a question to a specific person who has been quiet. "Do you have anything to add?" is a good follow-up question to ask another person. If the topic of conversation gets off track, move ahead by asking the next question in your study guide.

8. Before moving from questions to activities, ask group members if they have any questions that have not been answered. Remember that as a leader, you do not have to know all the answers. Some answers may come from group members. Other answers may even need a bit of research. Your

job is to keep the discussion moving and to encourage participation.

9. Review the activity in advance. Feel free to modify it or to create your own activity. Encourage participants to try the "at home" activity.

10. Following the conclusion of the activity, close with a brief prayer, praying either the printed prayer from the study guide or a prayer of your own. If your group desires, pause for individual prayer petitions.

11. Be grateful and supportive. Thank group members for their ideas and participation.

12. You are not expected to be a perfect leader. Just do the best you can by focusing on the participants and the lesson. God will help you lead this group.

13. Enjoy your time together!

SUGGESTIONS FOR PARTICIPANTS

1. What you will receive from this study will be in direct proportion to your involvement. Be an active participant!

2. Please make it a point to attend all sessions and to arrive on time so that you can receive the greatest benefit.

3. Read the chapter and review the study guide questions prior to the meeting. You may want to jot down questions you have from the reading, and also answers to some of the study-guide questions.

4. Be supportive and appreciative of your group leader as well as the other members of your group. You are on a journey together.

5. Your participation is encouraged. Feel free to share your thoughts about the material being discussed.

6. Pray for your group and your leader.

1. A Declaration of Dependence

SNAPSHOT SUMMARY

This chapter introduces the Beatitudes and shows why true happiness comes from making a personal commitment to live by their principles.

REFLECTION / DISCUSSION QUESTIONS

1. Share what you hope to gain from reading this book and exploring the Beatitudes.
2. What challenges are involved in understanding the Beatitudes?
3. How does living by the Beatitudes result in what the author refers to as "a declaration of dependence"?
4. Explain the problem with trying to define *happiness*.
5. Why does real happiness have nothing to do with chance?
6. Reflect on or discuss the connection between abundant life and character.
7. Reflect on or discuss what it means to be "owned by blessedness."
8. What are some of the blessings that come from our dependence upon God?
9. In your own words, explain why it takes courage to live according to the Beatitudes.
10. What additional insights or questions from this chapter would you like to explore?

ACTIVITIES

As a group: Brainstorm the topic of *happiness*. Together, create two lists, one containing thoughts about what happiness is, and another containing thoughts about what happiness is not. What truths are evident from these lists?

At home: Reflect upon your dependence on God. Consider how much and why you depend on God to shape your life and give you daily guidance.

Prayer: *Dear God, thank you for the Beatitudes and for this opportunity to learn about them. Help us guide our lives by Jesus' words and teachings, and remember that you are the source of true happiness. Amen.*

2. The Place, the People, and the Preacher

SNAPSHOT SUMMARY

This chapter provides more background into the Beatitudes, including where Jesus spoke them, his audience, and why he delivered his famous Sermon on the Mount.

REFLECTION / DISCUSSION QUESTIONS

1. Describe the followers and audience of Jesus at this point of his ministry.
2. What were some of the reasons people flocked to hear Jesus?
3. In what ways was the Sermon on the Mount both ordinary and extraordinary?
4. What is known about where the Sermon on the Mount was delivered?
5. Who was Jesus speaking to, and what was their reaction to his speech?

6. According to the author, what sets the Sermon on the Mount apart from other historically memorable speeches?

7. The author points out that the Sermon on the Mount was "not so much a sermon or a speech," as it was simply Jesus, the Teacher, "instructing a class." How is Jesus' teaching similar to or different from other teachings you have experienced?

8. What parallels or connections are there between Jesus' Sermon on the Mount and Moses' receiving the Ten Commandments?

9. Do you think the Beatitudes are more of a blessing, a challenge, or an inspiration? Explain your answer.

10. What additional insights or questions from this chapter would you like to explore?

ACTIVITIES

As a group: Create a list of what makes a sermon or a speech memorable. Talk about what you find most memorable from Jesus' Sermon on the Mount.

At home: Reflect on your openness to Jesus and his teachings. Think and pray about ways to open yourself more fully to following him. Prayerfully consider the truths of the Beatitudes and what your response to them will be.

Prayer: *Dear God, thank you for providing us with greater insights into the true meaning of happiness. Help us as we struggle to understand and accept the truths contained in Jesus' example and message. Amen.*

3. Poor and Happy

SNAPSHOT SUMMARY

This chapter looks at the connection between being *poor* and being *happy*, and it examines why true humility is hard to come by.

REFLECTION / DISCUSSION QUESTIONS

1. Share a time in your life when you were poor or felt poor. What feelings come to mind?
2. Reflect on or discuss the meaning of the phrase "poor in spirit."
3. Explain why the Jewish people in the time of Jesus might be described as "poor in spirit." What were the conditions under which they lived?
4. Reflect on or discuss how this Beatitude differs from the other Beatitudes, and how it serves, in a sense, as the foundation for the other Beatitudes that follow it.
5. What can we learn from this Beatitude and from this chapter regarding *humility*?
6. What is the connection between having true humility and giving up control? What would giving up control require in your life?
7. How is Jesus' parable of the Pharisee and tax collector almost a case study of this Beatitude?
8. What does this Beatitude reveal to us about the kingdom of heaven?
9. Why does the author say that this Beatitude "has a logic of its own"?
10. What additional insights or questions from this chapter would you like to explore?

ACTIVITIES

As a group: Work together to create a brief prayerful confession of poverty based upon insights gained from this chapter. Place your confession of poverty in a location where it can serve as a reminder of your need and your thankfulness.

At home: Reflect upon your own poverty and how you are personally challenged by this Beatitude.

Prayer: *Dear God, thank you for showing us the connection between poor and happy. Thank you for helping us see and admit our poverty, that through it we may draw closer to your son, Jesus Christ. Amen.*

4. The Happy Mourners

SNAPSHOT SUMMARY

This chapter looks at good reasons to mourn and the comfort and happiness that mourners can receive.

REFLECTION / DISCUSSION QUESTIONS

1. What are some of the circumstances that cause people to mourn?
2. Why do the words "happy mourners" seem to be a contradiction?
3. According to the author, what is one thing that may have been on Jesus' mind when he spoke this Beatitude?
4. According to the author, what were John Wesley's thoughts regarding this Beatitude?
5. Name some ways God and others minister to us in times of mourning.

6. What does this Beatitude have to say to those who mourn for others?
7. Why do people sometimes avoid or not assist those in deep mourning?
8. What does the author mean when he says, "Godly mourning makes for strength"?
9. Reflect on or discuss the blessings that can come from mourning.
10. What additional insights or questions from this chapter would you like to explore?

ACTIVITIES

As a group: Use the Bible to locate and discuss examples of happy mourners.

At home: Reflect upon ways you can act upon this Beatitude and make it a part of your daily life.

Prayer: *Dear God, thank you for reminding us of the connection between mourning and joy. Help us mourn for our own sins, help us bring strength and comfort to others, and may we seek to be faithful to you each day. Amen.*

5. The Meek Laugh Best

SNAPSHOT SUMMARY

This chapter explores what it means to be meek, how it takes strength to be gentle, and it shows us what Jesus meant when he said that the meek will "inherit the earth."

REFLECTION / DISCUSSION QUESTIONS

1. Reflect on or discuss the meaning of the word *meek* and how that term is perceived today.

2. What problems or challenges do people find with the statement that the meek will inherit the earth?

3. Why and in what ways do people try to avoid being labeled as *meek?*

4. Name some people found in the Bible who are described in terms of being meek.

5. Reflect on / discuss what William Barclay says about how this Beatitude could be translated, as "Blessed is the person who is always angry at the right time, and never angry at the wrong time."

6. According to the author, what is the secret of meekness?

7. Give some examples of meekness as seen in power that is under control.

8. According to the author, what are some of the specific ways in which the meek will inherit the earth?

9. Briefly describe someone you have known who has exemplified meekness.

10. What additional insights or questions from this chapter would you like to explore?

ACTIVITIES

As a group: Search current newspapers or magazines for examples of people who demonstrate meekness as it has been defined in this chapter.

At home: Consider how you can exemplify meekness in your own life.

Prayer: *Dear God, thank you for opening our eyes to what it means to be a meek person. Remind us that happiness comes in the restraint and disciplined use of whatever power we have. Amen.*

6. The Hunger Road to Happiness

SNAPSHOT SUMMARY

This chapter explores the topic of righteousness, along with the blessings and confidence received from hungering for it.

REFLECTION / DISCUSSION QUESTIONS

1. Share a time in your life when you experienced a hunger.
2. Explain what is meant by the idea that it is through hunger that we come to happiness.
3. Reflect on or discuss how people understood and experienced hunger in the time of Jesus. How is hunger generally understood and experienced by most of the people in the United States today?
4. Reflect on or discuss the meaning and the value of *righteousness*. Give an example of an act by a righteous person.
5. What did Jesus have in mind when he recommended a passionate hunger for righteousness?
6. What is the connection between happiness and righteousness?
7. According to the author, what are some reasons why people often don't thirst for *total* righteousness?
8. Give an example of how righteousness can be a "life-demanding, life-involving thing."
9. Reflect on or discuss the idea that when it comes to righteousness, "It is our hungering and thirsting that win the praise of our Lord, not our accomplishments."
10. What additional insights or questions from this chapter would you like to explore?

ACTIVITIES

As a group: Create a list of simple ways to implement this Beatitude each day.

At home: Reread this chapter and prayerfully reflect upon what it means to pursue righteousness. What steps can you take in your life to ensure that you are pursuing both personal and social righteousness?

Prayer: *Dear God, thank you for giving us a hunger and a thirst for total righteousness. Help us act bravely and unselfishly toward this goal, and thank you for lifting us up and renewing us when we become discouraged or feel that we have fallen short of the goal. Amen.*

7. Many Happy Returns

SNAPSHOT SUMMARY

This chapter looks at what it means to be merciful and how mercy brings mercy.

REFLECTION / DISCUSSION QUESTIONS

1. Describe some times in life during which people require mercy.
2. Name some reasons why people give mercy to others. Then name some reasons why people do not give mercy to others.
3. What lessons about mercy can be learned from Jesus' parable of the unforgiving servant (see Matthew 18:23-35)?
4. What does it mean when we say that there is a price tag attached to mercy?

5. In what ways can mercy be considered to require hard work?
6. What are some of the dangers or consequences of not showing mercy to others?
7. What do you think the author meant when he said, "Sometimes we think we're being merciful when we're only being muddleheaded"?
8. Share how you would define true Christian mercy.
9. Explain the connection between mercy and the title of this chapter, "Many Happy Returns."
10. What additional insights or questions from this chapter would you like to explore?

ACTIVITIES

As a group: Create a list with two columns, comparing both the costs and the benefits of being a merciful person.

At home: Prayerfully reflect on what it means to give and receive mercy. Practice being a merciful person.

Prayer: *Dear God, thank you for being merciful to us. Help us be merciful to others. Open our eyes to those in need of forgiveness and your love. Amen.*

8. Heartfelt Joy

SNAPSHOT SUMMARY

This chapter explores the happiness that belongs to the pure of heart and why they shall see God.

REFLECTION / DISCUSSION QUESTIONS

1. Name some situations where people experience joy.
2. Give your own definition of what it means to be pure of heart.

3. Explain why it can be difficult to be pure of heart in our culture. What are some of the challenges and obstacles?
4. Reflect on or discuss why purity often is not taken seriously today.
5. Where does purity exist in the world today? Who might be considered pure of heart?
6. Explain how and why the world actually *depends* upon the pure of heart.
7. What are some words that describe those who are pure of heart?
8. Reflect on or discuss how the pure of heart are able to see God.
9. How is purity of heart connected to the conscience?
10. What additional insights or questions from this chapter would you like to explore?

ACTIVITIES

As a group: Brainstorm ways in which people can possess and live out purity in today's world. If your time allows, let each member of the group write a short prayer asking God for a pure heart, and invite group members to share their prayers with the group.

At home: Reflect on and pray about what it means to be pure in heart. Examine your heart, your mind, and your life, and think about specific changes you may need to make. Ask God to give you a clean heart, that you may see God and comprehend.

Prayer: *Dear God, thank you for all that is pure in this world, for we know that it comes from our yearning after you. Help our words and deeds be pure in this life as we seek to reflect your goodness. Amen.*

9. A Very Happy Business

This chapter is about peace and peacemakers, and it explains why peacemakers are called the children of God.

REFLECTION / DISCUSSION QUESTIONS

1. How would you define *peace*?
2. Name some people or professions you might identify as peacemakers.
3. Give reasons why Jesus is known as the Prince of Peace. How did he promote peace? What does our world today need to learn from Jesus regarding peace?
4. Name some of the contributing factors toward lack of peace.
5. List some of the places and situations where peacemakers are needed today.
6. What qualities does it take to be a peacemaker?
7. Explain why peace must begin with individuals and come from within.
8. Reflect on or discuss the role and importance of communication in attaining and preserving peace.
9. Reflect on or discuss the role that prayer plays in peacemaking.
10. What additional insights or questions from this chapter would you like to explore?

ACTIVITIES

As a group: Create "personal statement" signs that encourage and promote peace—either world peace or inner peace.

At home: Pray for peace. Ask God to guide you in finding your role as a peacemaker.

Prayer: *Dear God, thank you for peace. Thank you for your Son, Jesus, the Prince of Peace, our Lord and our example. Help us be instruments of your peace in this world. Amen.*

10. Merry Martyrs

SNAPSHOT SUMMARY

This chapter explains the joys and rewards of those who are persecuted for their goodness and faithfulness to Jesus.

REFLECTION / DISCUSSION QUESTIONS

1. Share your initial reaction to this Beatitude.
2. Name some reasons why followers are persecuted for their commitment to Jesus Christ.
3. According to the author, what are the key phrases of this Beatitude, and why are they important?
4. Reflect on or discuss reasons why people are treated badly by others today. Is there a distinction between bad treatment and persecution? Give reasons for your answer.
5. Name some of the many forms persecution can take.
6. What dangers and consequences exist for those who stand by their convictions?
7. How and why do people *avoid* persecution?
8. Name some places where Christians are persecuted today. What are your thoughts on how Christians in the United States today are viewed or treated by others? Explain your answers.
9. What does it mean to find the happiness in perse-

cution? What is the blessing for suffering in the name of the Lord?
10. What additional insights or questions from this chapter would you like to explore?

ACTIVITIES

As a group: Use the Bible to locate and discuss examples of persecution of early Christians.

At home: Reflect upon why you are or are not persecuted for your faith. What evidence is there that you are a follower of Jesus?

Prayer: *Dear God, thank you for giving us the courage to face all of the challenges in life. Help us not turn away from persecution, but deal with it as Christians. Help us reflect your goodness and allow your love and presence to show in our lives. Amen.*

11. So Where Do We Begin?

SNAPSHOT SUMMARY

This chapter looks back at what has been covered and then looks ahead at ways to apply the Beatitudes to daily life.

REFLECTION / DISCUSSION QUESTIONS

1. In what ways might the Beatitudes be said to run contrary to common sense?
2. What do you think Jesus had in mind in giving us the Beatitudes?
3. Which Beatitude is the most difficult for you to understand or practice? Why is that?

4. Reflect on or discuss the following statement: "God expects us—those of us who take Jesus seriously—to make as much of a difference as is within our reach."

5. Reflect on or discuss the pros and cons of what the author identifies as a key word, *happy*. What is the distinction between happiness and joy?

6. Discuss how the "Beatitude person" sees life and is different.

7. How can sources of distress actually be settings for happiness?

8. Discuss the role self-esteem plays in how we live and in our degree of happiness.

9. Present your case for why the Beatitudes represent the only practical way to live.

10. Share where you want to go from here. What changes would you like to make in your life?

ACTIVITIES

As a group: Create a group list of ten ways to live the Beatitudes. Make copies of the list for each group member to keep.

At home: Prayerfully reflect upon where you want to go from here and how you wish to change your life. Give thanks for God's patience and love; for the teachings, example, and love of Jesus Christ; and for the caring, love, and support of family and friends.

Prayer: *Dear God, thank you for this time together and for the learning, sharing, and growth that have taken place. Grant that the Beatitudes may have a special place in our lives and that our lives will be changed because of this experience. Amen.*

NOTES

1. A DECLARATION OF DEPENDENCE

1. Henry C. Link, *The Return to Religion* (New York: Macmillan Company, 1936), 168, 169.
2. William Barclay, *The Gospel of Matthew,* vol. 1 (Philadelphia: Westminster Press, 1958), 84.
3. C. S. Lewis, *Surprised by Joy* (New York: Harcourt, Brace and Company, 1955), 3.
4. Barclay, *The Gospel of Matthew,* 83.
5. *The Random House Dictionary of the English Language* (New York: Random House, 1966), 131.

2. THE PLACE, THE PEOPLE, AND THE PREACHER

1. Johnson Oatman, Jr., "Higher Ground," *Favorite Hymns of Praise* (Chicago: Tabernacle Publishing Company, 1972), 262.
2. Thomas C. Oden, editor, *Ancient Christian Commentary on Scripture,* vol. 1a (Downers Grove, Ill.: InterVarsity Press, 2001), 77.

3. POOR AND HAPPY

1. *The Interpreter's Bible,* vol. 7 (New York: Abingdon-Cokesbury, 1951), 280.
2. Eugene H. Peterson, W*here Your Treasure Is;* quoted in Eugene H. Peterson, *God's Message for Each Day* (Nashville: J. Countryman, 2004), 289.
3. *The United Methodist Hymnal* (Nashville: The United Methodist Publishing House, 1989), 12.

4. THE HAPPY MOURNERS

1. J. B. Phillips, *Is God at Home?* (Nashville: Abingdon Press, 1957), 24.
2. William Barclay, *The Gospel of Matthew,* vol. 1 (Philadelphia: Westminster Press, 1958), 88.
3. Henry C. Link, *The Return to Religion* (New York: Macmillan Company, 1936), 178-79.

5. THE MEEK LAUGH BEST

1. Gordon Powell, *Happiness Is a Habit* (Carmel, N.Y.: Guidepost Associates, 1967), 31.
2. Harold Myra and Marshall Shelley, *The Leadership Secrets of Billy Graham* (Grand Rapids: Zondervan, 2005), 196.
3. William Barclay, *The Gospel of Matthew,* vol. 1 (Philadelphia: Westminster Press, 1958), 91.
4. Ralph W. Sockman, *The Higher Happiness* (New York: Abingdon-Cokesbury Press, 1950), 71-72.

6. THE HUNGER ROAD TO HAPPINESS

1. Ralph W. Sockman, *The Higher Happiness* (New York: Abingdon-Cokesbury Press, 1950), 95.

7. MANY HAPPY RETURNS

1. Ralph W. Sockman, *The Higher Happiness* (New York: Abingdon-Cokesbury Press, 1950), 98.
2. William Barclay, *The Gospel of Matthew,* vol. 1 (Philadelphia: Westminster Press, 1958), 98.
3. Billy Graham, *The Secret of Happiness* (Garden City, N.Y.: Doubleday, 1955), 62.

8. HEARTFELT JOY

1. Brian Doyle, *The Wet Engine* (Brewster, Mass.: Paraclete Press, 2005), 20, 84, 87.
2. Ibid., 15.
3. William Barclay, *The Gospel of Matthew* (Philadelphia: The Westminster Press, 1958), vol. 1, 101-102.
4. Ralph W. Sockman, *The Higher Happiness* (New York: Abingdon-Cokesbury Press, 1950), 118.
5. Leonard Griffith, *Pathways to Happiness* (New York: Abingdon Press, 1964), 94.
6. Helen H. Lemmel, "Turn Your Eyes upon Jesus," *The United Methodist Hymnal* (Nashville: The United Methodist Publishing House, 1989), #349.

9. A VERY HAPPY BUSINESS

1. Arthur Compton, "The Day That Changed Your Life," *Guideposts* 17, no. 1 (March 1962): 3.
2. Joseph Stein, *Fiddler on the Roof* (New York: Crown Publishers, 1965), 107.
3. William Barclay, *The Gospel of Matthew,* vol. 1 (Philadelphia: Westminster Press, 1958), 103.
4. *The Interpreter's Bible* (Nashville: Abingdon-Cokesbury Press, 1951), vol. 7, 286.

5. Ralph W. Sockman, *The Higher Happiness* (New York: Abingdon-Cokesbury Press, 1950), 148.
6. Henry C. Link, *The Return to Religion* (New York: Macmillan Company, 1936), 130-31.

10. MERRY MARTYRS

1. William Barclay, *The Gospel of Matthew,* vol. 1 (Philadelphia: Westminster Press, 1958), 112.
2. Ralph W. Sockman, *The Higher Happiness* (New York: Abingdon-Cokesbury Press, 1950), 155.
3. William E. Sangster, *He Is Able* (Nashville: Cokesbury Press, 1937), 78-79.
4. C. Milo Connick, *Build on the Rock* (Westwood, N.J.: Revell, 1960), 47.

11. SO WHERE DO WE BEGIN?

1. Craig Lambert, "The Science of Happiness," *Harvard Magazine* 109, no. 3 (January-February 2007): 29.
2. Molly Bruce Jacobs, "My (Secret) Sister," *AARP* 49, no. 1C (January-February 2006): 58.
3. J. B. Phillips, *Day by Day with J. B. Phillips*, ed. Denis Duncan (Peabody, Mass.: Hendrickson Publishers, 2003), 204.
4. Quoted in *Christian Century* 121, no. 13 (June 29, 2004): 7.
5. G. A. Studdert-Kennedy, *The Best of G. A. Studdert-Kennedy* (London: Hodder & Stoughton, 1951), 119.
6. Stephen H. Webb, "The Path Less Beaten: Jack Kerouac's *On the Road,*" *Touchstone* 18, no. 8 (October 2005): 14-16.